WORLD WAR 2

For Young Readers

EF Clark

EF Clark Publishing
www.efclark.com

Recommended for ages 12+

The Root of War

Nations from all over the planet sent soldiers to fight in World War 2

It's estimated that as many as 100 million people died as a result of the deadliest war in human history. It was called World War 2.

New frightening weapons were created and nations from all over the planet enlisted soldiers to fight in the conflict, including Germany, Japan, Italy, France, Russia, China, England, Australia, Canada, Brazil, and America.

Establishing a time when the war started is difficult. Some historians say World War 2 was really an extension of World War 1 because many of the same nations were pitted against each other again.

Japan, Italy, and Germany invaded others nations as early as 1931. The Spanish Civil War from 1936-1939 was supported by nations that later were involved in World War 2, including Germany, Russia, and Mexico.

To understand what started this terrible conflict, we must try to realize how things were different than they are today.

Language barriers, distance, and cultural diversity have always separated citizens of the different nations. But in the early part of the 20th century, the great empires and kingdoms that were so powerful in the past had begun to change.

Revolutions and the election of leaders with new ideas meant the old way of doing things were quickly becoming outdated. **Dictators** were defining the new century with bold ideas of global control.

In 1917, at the end of World War 1, Russia became the Soviet Union as it fell to communists led by a dictator named Lenin.

Define

DICTATOR

A leader with total control and power over others

The United States emerged from the First World War as a major global force for the first time. And Germany had suffered a terrible loss.

After World War 1 ended with Germany's defeat in 1918, the U.S. became the greatest economic and military power in the world.

World War One era German bi-plane

Germany suffered the shame of losing the war as well as being economically devastated. Germans were in need of leaders who could restore their honor, and their financial system.

Hitler Comes to Power

Adolf Hitler had been a soldier in the First World War. By the early 1920s he was the leader of Germany's National Socialist Party, or *Nazi* for short.

From then on, the Nazis pushed hard to spread their message of "hope" and power to the nation. With the shame of defeat in the First World War and such great poverty in Germany, many citizens welcomed the message.

Adolf Hitler's Nazi party was also called the **Third Reich**, or empire. The first two empires were the Roman Empire and Imperial Germany.

Nazis in Germany began to build a strong army with all types of weapons and impressive uniforms, giving them a sense of honor among the people. They also used symbols, flags, and parades to excite the German people into joining them.

Adolf Hitler celebrates becoming Chancellor of Germany, January 1933

As Hitler and the Nazi Party became more powerful, they caused fear and told lies about anyone who opposed them.

Jewish people became the main target in Hitler's plan to take control of Germany.
The Nazis used the Jews to get Germans on their side. False rumors were spread that the Jewish people were to blame for all of Germany's problems.

After Adolf Hitler came to absolute power as the Chancellor of Germany in January of 1933, the Nazi Party quickly began making new laws against Jewish citizens and Jewish business owners.

With his great ability to speak to large crowds, Germany's new "**Führer**" (leader) convinced Germans that their destiny was to rule the world.

The first thing they must do, Hitler told them, was to get rid of the Jews. Before long it became apparent that the "camps" built for Jews were really prisons where millions of innocent people would die.

Hitler's Nazi Germany would in time make agreements with Italy and Japan to defend one other. The three nations would be called the "**Axis Powers**".

Adolf Hitler with members of the early Nazi Party

On the other side of the planet, Japan took steps to control Asia. The Japanese prepared for war against China by amassing a mighty army and navy.

With the Axis Powers eager to take control of Europe and Asia, the stage was set for another world war.

The United States kept a close eye on the events in Europe and Asia. In the early 1930s the USA had enough problems of its own without getting into another war. After the First World War, most Americans just wanted to maintain peace.

In October of 1929, the **Great Depression** had begun. The economic collapse of the Wall Street stock market crippled America, and most people struggled to make ends meet. Americans were desperate to forget about their worries.

Define
GREAT DEPRESSION
A tough worldwide economic condition

Motion pictures, or movies as they're called today, were a great way for people to escape from their troubles.

In the 1930s, a movie ticket only cost about 25¢ but that was a lot when one in four Americans were out of work.

BROOKLYN DAILY EAGLE

And Complete Long Island News

LATE NEWS

WALL ST. IN PANIC AS STOCKS CRASH

Attempt Made to Kill Italy's Crown Prince

ASSASSIN CAUGHT IN BRUSSELS MOB; PRINCE UNHURT

Hollywood Fire Destroys Films Worth Millions

FEAR 52 PERISHED IN LAKE MICHIGAN; FERRY IS MISSING

PIECE OF PLANE LIKE DITEMAN'S IS FOUND AT SEA

High Duty Group Gave $700,000 to Coolidge Drive

STOCKS CRASH IN RUSH TO SELL; BILLIONS LOST

Before the movie started, theatres would play short "newsreels" to inform the audience about world events. Many Americans learned about Hitler and the Nazis by watching newsreels. They also learned about what was happening in Asia.

The newsreels, as well as radio reports and newspaper articles let people all over America know about the plans of the Axis powers.

Although it was obvious that Hitler was gearing for war, most Americans wanted to stay out of it. As the Nazis began expanding their borders into other countries, the United States waited to see what would happen.

Other nations in Europe, however, felt that they did not have the luxury to simply watch and do nothing. England and France were very concerned about Hitler's power grab.

A World at War

Then, in July of 1937, Japanese forces invaded China. The Japanese wanted to capture vast Chinese resources to make their own country stronger.

Under the leadership of President **Franklin Delano Roosevelt**, the United States government took action against Japan for the attack. The U.S. cut off all shipments of oil, iron, and other raw materials. Japan saw this as an act of war because most of Japan's oil came from the USA.

At first **Emperor Hirohito**, the leader of Japan, was more concerned about the Soviet Union than America because they had been at war with Russia before.

Hirohito and his top advisors did not think the United States would pose a threat to their plans of expansion.

As Japanese forces landed on mainland Asia, the U. S. and Russia had a common concern. But Japan chose to take the risk. After all, **Japan** had the third most powerful navy in the world. The Chinese struggled to fight back, but it was no use.

Emperor Hirohito of Japan

The following year, in 1938, **Neville Chamberlain,** the leader of England, and Édouard Daladier of France visited Adolf Hitler and the Italian leader, Benito Mussolini. They met in Munich, Germany to discuss keeping the peace.

After a few other meetings with Hitler, Chamberlain went home to Great Britain convinced that there would be no war between the nations.

But other leaders in England, such as Winston Churchill believed it was only a matter of time before Germany's quest for power would lead to war in Europe.

In Germany, the persecution of Jews continued. Late in 1938, the world was shocked to hear about an event named **Kristallnacht** (German for "crystal night").

In one night alone, special Nazi soldiers called *stormtroopers* destroyed or damaged over 1,000 Jewish houses of worship (synagogues) and 7,000 Jewish businesses. 30,000 Jewish people were arrested and nearly 100 were killed. Jewish homes and schools were also raided.

Kristallnacht was named for the all the glass that littered the streets after windows were broken, but the Nazi's reign of terror had only begun.

Jewish Synagogue in Berlin the day after Kristallnacht

When the Nazis broke a treaty called the Munich Agreement by invading nearby provinces belonging to other countries in March of 1939, Chamberlain tried again to keep the peace.

This time, he met with leaders from France and **Joseph Stalin**, the leader of the Soviet Union who had taken Lenin's place. Stalin was a dictator much like Hitler himself.

Comparing him to historical dictators like Napoleon, French Prime Minister **Édouard Daladier** understood Adolf Hitler's aim. Nazi Germany desired to rule the continent of Europe and capture slaves to work for them.

ABOVE: German forces attack Poland, September 1st, 1939

Because of the fertile farmland found in **Poland**, Daladier believed Germany's next move would be to invade its neighbor to the east.

Agreeing to draw the line against Hitler, Chamberlain and Daladier warned Germany that an attack on Poland would mean war with England and France.

Meanwhile, Prime Minister Chamberlain's talks with Joseph Stalin were not going well. The communist leader was not to be trusted.

In September 1939 any hope of peace was shattered when the Soviet Union joined forces with

Germany and attacked **Poland**, Germany from the west and the Russians from the east. England and France knew war had begun.

Even though outnumbered in troops, tanks, and aircraft, the Polish armed forces fought the invasion bravely.

Germany lost 25% of its planes in a weeklong struggle. Despite the noble Polish resistance, the nation's fate was sealed when the Soviet Union attacked on September 17th.

With the French leader's worst fear a reality, England and France had to follow up on their promise to Poland. On September 3rd, two days after the attack, England and France, the **Allies**, declared war on Germany.

Nazi troops remove a barrier at the border of Germany and Poland

However, neither France nor England reacted militarily. The Polish people felt betrayed, not only by the brutal attack, but by her Western allies as well. Once the Nazis had control of Poland, they began taking prisoners.

People that were not even in the army were captured as well. All of the Jews were rounded up and put into camps. The camps were crowded and dirty. Many of the prisoners were beaten and starved, and many died of abuse and disease.

Throughout World War 2, Germany continued to arrest, persecute, and mistreat Jewish people in Eastern Europe.

The Phoney War

With France and Britain now in the war, the German high command planned their strategy. France was in danger of attack because it shared a border with Germany. Each nation waited for the other to make a move.

England also tried to come up with a way to stop the Nazis. All the countries in Europe were on high alert.

British warplanes prepared to defend against a possible invasion. When the Soviet Union attacked Finland in November 1939, many people in Northern Europe were afraid and confused.

Across the Atlantic Ocean, President Franklin Roosevelt became more involved in taking sides with the Allies. Both England and France looked to America to supply them with weapons, aircraft, and tanks.

Still, through the winter of 1939 and 1940, no major conflict occurred. This was called "the Phoney

War" because of the standoff. But everything was about to change.

Define
U-BOAT
German Submarines named "undersea boats"

Early in 1940, action began to heat up in the icy waters of the North Atlantic Ocean. The Soviet Union began a series of fierce battles with Finland. German submarines, called **U-boats** stepped up assault against allied ships.

Because two oceans isolated the United States, most Americans did not feel the effects of the war. Europe and Asia were tangled in combat, but America was far away from the fighting.

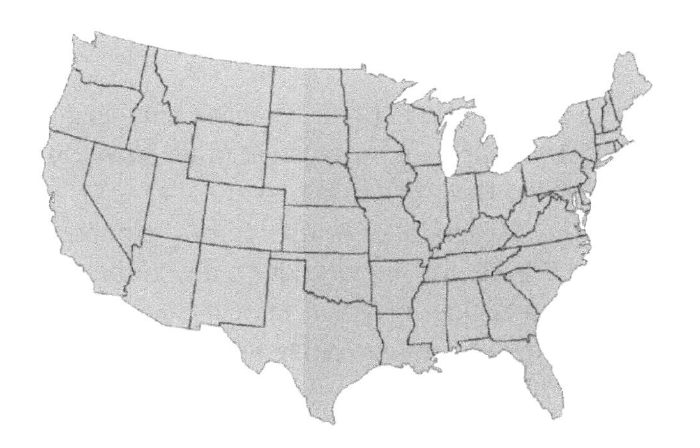

As the hunger for power grew among the Axis Powers, Hitler set his sights on the north. Despite promises that no attack would happen, Norway and Denmark fell in the spring of 1940.

With the heavy use of their air force, the **Luftwaffe** (German for "air weapon"), Nazi invaders crushed the Dutch military quickly.

The Battle of the Netherlands lasted less than a week. After intense fighting to defend their homeland, the nation of Norway also surrendered to Nazi Germany in early May.

The Battle of France

For the first time, France and England entered the war in an important way. Now Hitler knew that the Nazis had to act fast.

The French and British forces grouped in northern France. Moving quickly to divide them, the Nazi war machine invaded French soil, charging between the two armies from behind.

The Battle of France Marked the First Tank Battle in the War

Miles of Nazi armored vehicles raced through the **Ardennes Forest** and circled around to surprise the Allies. It was a risky move, but Hitler gambled on a surprise attack. The Nazis had become good at moving a large army with extraordinary speed and efficiency.

The French were sure the attack would come from a different place and were caught off guard by the Nazi **Blitzkrieg** (German for "lightning war").

A Nazi tank rolls through the Ardennes Forest in France, May 1940

The Battle of France would mark the first tank battle in the European war. With their backs to the **English Channel**, the British forces were almost forced to surrender. But the order was given from the German high command to slow the attack.

This gave Winston Churchill, the new leader of England, a chance to pull his troops out.

With the German decision to slow down, the English troops fell back to **Dunkirk**, a coastal town in northern France near the Belgian border.

From the Strait of Dover beach at Dunkirk, only 21 miles of water divides England from mainland Europe.

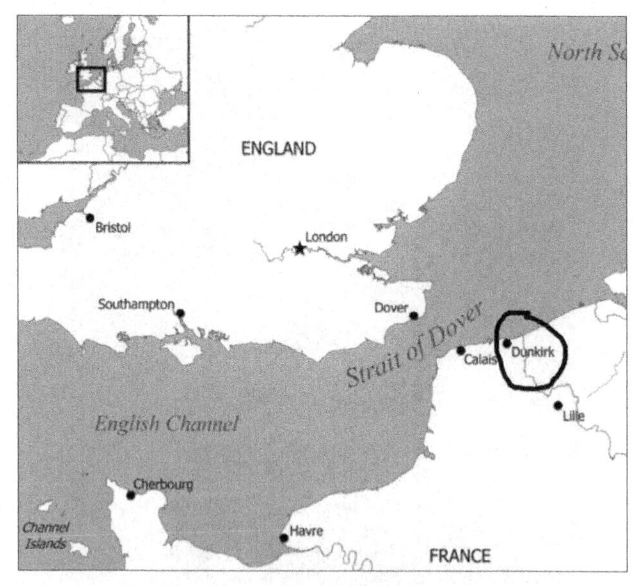

Unknown to the Germans, the British War Department had decided to retreat. From May 27th to June 4th over 300,000 men were evacuated from Dunkirk. It was one of the boldest acts of the war.

Losses of ships and airplanes were high on both sides. Even though they lost the Battle of Dunkirk, the retreat gave the British the will to fight another day.

At great risk, the retreat was made possible in part to the bravery of regular people. Many "little boats" belonging to private citizens were used to cross the channel for the rescue.

The Battle of Dunkirk had shown the British people that they could come together for the good of the nation. The Germans had lost a good chance to defeat England at Dunkirk.

Left behind on the beach by the British army were enormous amounts of guns and bullets, as well as almost 700 tanks and about 65,000 other vehicles.

Exhausted British soldiers preparing for retreat at Dunkirk

Under the cover of darkness, the last of the Allied troops were rescued from Dunkirk with the German forces only two miles away. Prime Minister Churchill called it a *"miracle of deliverance"* and vowed to never surrender.

Much of the equipment the British left was destroyed to keep it from being used by the enemy.

The remaining French soldiers were now forced to retreat. Falling back further into their homeland, they were pursued by the devastating German "Blitzkrieg". French military leaders were caught off guard by the speed of Germany's armored division.

The world watched as a new kind of warfare unfolded. German citizens were thrilled at the heroic adventure of their young soldiers under the **Führer**.

Within weeks, Italy declared war on England and France. Nazi pressure was being felt around the world, as far away as South America and Arab countries like Iraq. And Japanese forces continued to push deeper into Asia.

World War 2 was spreading quickly like wild fire. Everywhere around the planet, news of the war made headlines.

THIS WORLD TODAY

San Francisco Chronicle

The City's Only Home-Owned Newspaper

Million Nazis in Northern Reich, Holland, Denmark Surrender; 500,000 Remain in the Fight

Big Four Confer

Unity Indicated; Molotov May Leave Tomorrow

The Story of A Picture and An Editorial . .

Jap Air, Sea Battle

Five Light U. S. Warships Sunk Off Okinawa

Broken Bonds---Broken Armies

Enemy Flees Under Allied Aerial Scourge: Liberated Danes Sing and Shout in Streets

Mobilization Of Patriots

Negotiations Are Reported Now On for Capitulation

Everywhere around the planet, news of the war made headlines

Even as the terrible events sent shockwaves all over the United States, most Americans were not prepared to send troops to another distant war to fight and die.

From the farms to the cities to the universities, Americans enjoyed peace within their borders. Life went on as it had before all the battles started. Still, the news was hard to avoid. **Radio** was the main method of communication.

Radio kept Americans up to date with reports from around the world. Every week, millions of people from all over the nation listened to music, and other forms of entertainment, as well as President Roosevelt's "fireside chats," a way the president informed the people of America with a hopeful message.

In the days before Internet video and even TV, Americans listened to radios at home, in their cars, and at work. Radio broadcasts kept the American public aware of Germany and Japan's moves.

The war seemed far away to most listeners. But for Roosevelt and his top advisers, it was closer than they wanted to admit. Hitler's plans, along with the Japanese expansion, meant America could not sit out of the war for long. As America listened, the news only got worse.

Under the command of General **Erwin Rommel**, the armored tank invasion of France pushed on. The Nazi leader displayed intelligence and courage, as the French were quickly beat back.

Hitler was impressed with Rommel's squadron, which became known as "the Ghost Squadron" because of the speed they were able to advance.

Although the French fought hard to defend their cities, one by one they fell into Rommel's hands. Aided by the **Luftwaffe**, the Nazi general stormed toward Paris.

Unable to resist the German assault, France had no choice but to surrender. Soon after, Hitler arrived in Paris to pose under the **Eiffel Tower**.

France had no Choice but to Surrender

On June 21st, 1940 the Germans demanded the French to sign a peace treaty in Paris. The event was designed as revenge for Germany's disgrace after World War One.

French leaders were ordered to sign the treaty in the same railroad car that was used when Germany surrendered after the First World War. The car was brought from a museum for the event.

That same month, Nazi **Gestapo** officials began filling Auschwitz Concentration Camp in Poland with Jewish prisoners, where millions would eventually die.

Define
GESTAPO
Nazi Germany's secret police, created to scare Hitler's enemies

As Italy and Japan united with Nazi Germany, other countries such as Canada, Australia, New Zealand, and South Africa also entered the war on the Allied side.

After the Nazi victory in France, Adolf Hitler began to prepare for the invasion of England. The plan called for massive air raids of British industry and residential areas.

German Focke-Wulf Fw 190 fighter aircraft

The European war would soon reach a level of destructive firepower that no one could have believed.

Fueled by the desire to conquer Britain, Hitler was willing to do whatever it took to defeat his foe. To survive, England needed a brave new leader.

Winston Churchill was just the kind of leader that Great Britain needed to face such a dark time in history.

Never before in England's history had the people been so alarmed. And never before had they put so much hope in one man. The English people showed courage in the face of war. But soon they would learn the cost of defending their nation would be much greater than they could have imagined.

Throughout the summer of 1940, the British waited and watched for any sign of German movement in the skies and on the sea.

A British scout stands on a rooftop in London scanning the sky for enemy aircraft.

The Battle of Britain

The Nazis had made astonishing advances in the war. They overran the Netherlands and Belgium in just a few short weeks. German military strategy had proven to be superior and, although better equipped, the British and French were caught off guard at Dunkirk.

At the beginning of the war in Europe, no other country seemed more ready for combat than Nazi Germany.

Hitler had faith that his military leaders could win the war against the Allies and he would rule the world.

The Reichsadler (the Nazi coat of arms)

With the rapid victories in Poland, Norway, Holland, and France, it seemed that nothing could stop the Nazi war machine from taking control of Europe. Hitler had devised a sinister plan and would stop at nothing to gain absolute power.

However, as Nazi generals and admirals began drawing plans for the invasion of Great Britain, Hitler underestimated his enemy across the English Channel.

The terrible memories of the First World War caused England to avoid another war with Germany. British Prime Minister Neville Chamberlain had done all he could to keep the peace.

Nazi poster showing Stuka dive-bombers over England

Hitler underestimated the British

As the new prime minister, Churchill had sent troops to France only to have them retreat at Dunkirk. Now, with the threat of a Nazi German attack, the British relied on a new tool called **Radar** for defense.

> Define
> ***RADAR***
>
> Stands for **RA**dio **D**etection **A**nd **R**anging

Radar uses radio waves to detect airplanes miles away from the towers that send the signal back.

In 1904, German inventor Christian Hülsmeyer first used radio waves to detect metal objects.

Before World War 2, many nations, including the United States, Germany, Japan, and Russia, were secretly working to develop radar.

The British were the first to use radar in the war. Nazi Germany had radar, but they had not yet used it to defend their borders.

Military planners in both Germany and England knew the importance of radar. They also knew that the location of the towers must be kept a secret. In conjunction with other defensive measures, radar would play a crucial role in the Battle of Britain.

The War Expands

The Mediterranean Sea, between Italy and the northern coast of Africa

In June of 1940, German submarines continued to sink British merchant ships in the North Atlantic.

The British submarine HMS Odin attacked two Italian war ships in the first naval battle in the **Mediterranean Sea**. The Odin was sunk in the conflict.

For the first time, an American warship, the Destroyer USS Dickerson, cruised into a port in Europe as a safety measure. President Roosevelt put the War Department on alert.

Even though the British trusted Winston Churchill to lead them into victory, the mood of the nation was gloomy. Times were about to get even worse.

In the summer of 1940, the English government warned citizens not to go the beaches. All horse racing was stopped by the British Jockey Club.

England began preparing for an invasion by urging the people to "black out" the lights in windows at night. Putting heavy dark drapes on their windows would prevent German aircraft from finding the cities.

Adolf Hitler and Benito Mussolini together in Munich, Germany, June 1940

German and Italian military leaders were glad to see the war going their way. Certain that the plans for the Battle of Britain were being drawn up, Churchill prepared for the worst.

As a precaution, over 100,000 British children were moved west, away from the likely area of attack. British radar operators were called to high alert. The British defense system worked well and would save many lives.

Citizen soldiers patrolled the streets with binoculars watching for any sign of Nazi warplanes. No one knew when the invasion would come, but everyone was told to be ready.

German bombers raiding England, July 1940

On July 1st, the first phase of the German invasion of Britain began. It was called **Operation Sea Lion**.

Nazi planes bombed British factories in Hull, England and Wick, Scotland. Soon, the skies would be darkened by hundreds of Nazi planes.

Hitler was certain the British would surrender, but Churchill remained defiant, calling for his people to *"never yield to the apparently overwhelming might of the enemy"*.

The sheer willpower on both sides meant a long, bloody battle was sure to take place.

In response to the German raid on England, British leaders launched an attack of their own. On July 5th, 1940 British bombers rained explosives down on two German cities.

British Royal Air Force Spitfire fighters defending the homeland, 1940

Taking their **Spitfire** airplanes to the skies over the English Channel, Royal Air Force (RAF) pilots started a routine of intercepting incoming German attackers.

Destined to be one of the great fighter planes of the Second World War, the Spitfire and the brave pilots of the RAF became legendary.

Five days later, another famous warplane was introduced. The Japanese A6M **Zero** went into action against the Chinese.

World War 2 raged like no other conflict before or since, on the ground, at sea, and in the air. But the British were only just beginning to feel the brutality of Hitler's blitz. The Battle of Britain would be one of the longest in the war.

Royal Air Force Pilots and their Spitfires became Legendary

"Never in the field of human conflict was so much owed by so many to so few"

-Winston Churchill,
speaking of the bravery of RAF pilots

The London Blitz

As the summer dragged on, Nazi bombings of Britain became more severe.

The **Luftwaffe** damaged many buildings but was also losing numerous airplanes. Hitler's top generals were planning a ground invasion of England for mid-August, but the losses made them rethink their strategy.

At the same time, British bombers regularly attacked German factories and cities, making Hitler angry. In revenge, the Nazi air force commenced what was known as "The London Blitz".

In early September 1940 the Luftwaffe heavily bombed England every night for almost two months. From France, German long-range guns began shelling Southern England as well. The attack on England continued for over eight months.

Fear gripped the heart of London as thousands gathered each night in underground shelters to avoid danger.

More than one million homes in Britain were destroyed or damaged. Over 40,000 people were killed. Still, Germany failed to break the spirit of the British people.

They also missed the chance to destroy important targets, like **radar** towers.

Frustrated by the failed plan, the Nazis would finally give up the idea of a land attack on Britain. The plan was simply too costly to succeed.

Adolf Hitler and his top air force commander Hermann Goring

President Roosevelt and his top advisers eagerly watched the Blitz take its toll. Americans began to change their minds about the war. Congress voted to spend more money to update the military.

Many of the ships, tanks, airplanes, and other weapons had not been upgraded since the First World War ended in 1918.

Henry Ford at the construction site of Willow Run Aircraft factory located in Michigan

American automakers like **Henry Ford** were contracted to build new aircraft for the U.S. Army. Ford put car production on hold and constructed the Willow Run aircraft plant. Over a mile long, the plant eventually produced a B24 bomber every 60 minutes, 24 hours a day, 7 days a week.

The London Blitz, along with the arrest, torture, and murder of millions of **civilians** by the Nazis and Japanese, was a turning point for the United States.

Many Americans began thinking they could no longer ignore the war.

Still, most Americans didn't truly understand the suffering that the war was causing around the world.

Define

CIVILIAN

People who are not in the military

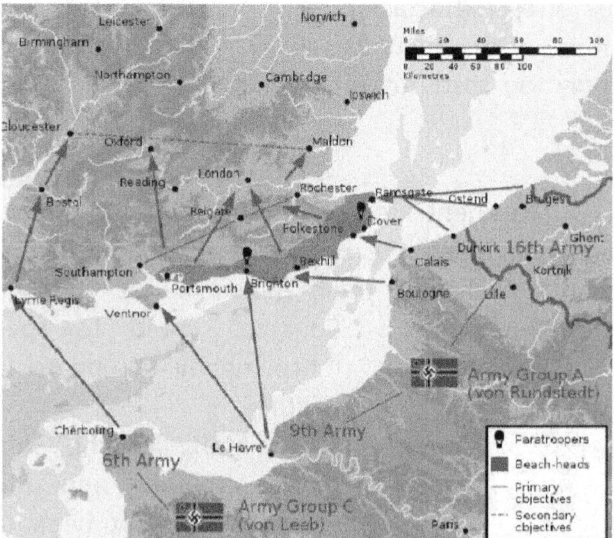

"Operation Sea Lion" was the German plan to invade England in 1940

The demand on England to fight the Italians in the Mediterranean and defend their shores from German attacks put a heavy burden on the soldiers and sailors. But, with the help of Canada and others, the will to fight remained strong.

Soon most of the globe would be in a firestorm. The entire world's industry would be geared to fight the war. One by one, the nations chose sides. Very few would remain neutral.

Germany, Italy, and Japan signed a treaty to defend each other. Korea, Romania, Finland, Libya, and Thailand also joined the Axis Powers.

Japanese children celebrating the Treaty with Germany and Italy, 1940

Even though losing France as an ally made it harder to fight Axis Powers, England had the aid of other nations. The United States, Canada, Greece, Australia, Egypt, and many more helped in different ways.

Plus, there was still an important force in Europe, the French Resistance, or Free France. Free France was a group of armed forces led by French General **Charles De Gaulle**, a stubborn and proud patriot. Refusing to surrender, De Gaulle fled France when the Nazis attacked.

Churchill and DeGaulle

Winston Churchill allowed De Gaulle to operate inside of Britain during the Nazi siege of France.

At first General De Gaulle's challenge to his fellow countrymen to rise up against the Nazis didn't go well. But by the end of the war, Free France had become the 4th largest Allied army in Europe.

With De Gaulle's determination, Free France grew. The French Resistance would expand to over one million soldiers as Frenchmen were freed from Nazi rule. They fought in a variety of battles and locations, including the liberation of Paris.

LEFT: French Resistance fighters planning attacks on Nazi convoys.

INTERNATIONAL CONFLICT

Victorious Japanese soldiers march into Beijing, China

As war raged in Europe, the conflict continued to expand in Asia. Japanese forces captured Vietnam and French Indochina.

In addition to all the other global conflicts, Chinese armies continued to fight each other. Nationalist and communist forces faced off in the ongoing Chinese Civil War. After World War 2, the communist forces would finally come to power.

Even as the Japanese imposed their power in Asia, Italy and Germany would push the war onto a new continent.

When Italian dictator Benito Mussolini ordered his forces to invade Egypt in September 1940, he dreamed of rebuilding the ancient Roman Empire.

In the land of the great pyramids, Mussolini wanted what Julius Caesar sought to conquer 2,000 years earlier.

New frontiers were quickly opening as World War 2 spilled across national borders and continental boundaries. On nearly all horizons, warplanes crowded the skies over the great cities of the world.

Never before or since would humanity witness a war that would spread so fast to so many places on the planet.

Italian dictator Mussolini ordered his forces to invade Egypt in 1940

The Nazis also had their eyes on the African continent. Slave labor would be in abundance. Vast natural resources like oil and metals could supply the German war factories.

Italian and British tanks clashed for the rest of 1940 in the deserts of Northern Africa. In February 1941 Hitler sent one of his favorite generals, Erwin Rommel to lead the **Afrika Korps.**

ABOVE: Tank warfare between the British and Germans in Northern Africa

All along the southern coast of the Mediterranean Sea from the Middle East to the Atlantic Ocean, African nations became the battlefield of modern warfare. Important battles would be decided in Egypt, Libya, Tunisia, Algeria, and Morocco across the Sahara Desert.

When **General Rommel** arrived in early 1941, his mission was to support the Italian forces and prevent a retreat from the British offensive. Italy had occupied Ethiopia and other territories in Eastern Africa since 1936. But local rebel uprising, rough desert conditions, and now British attacks had slowed the progress of Mussolini's plans. General Rommel would be effective in slowing the British offensive, but it wouldn't be easy.

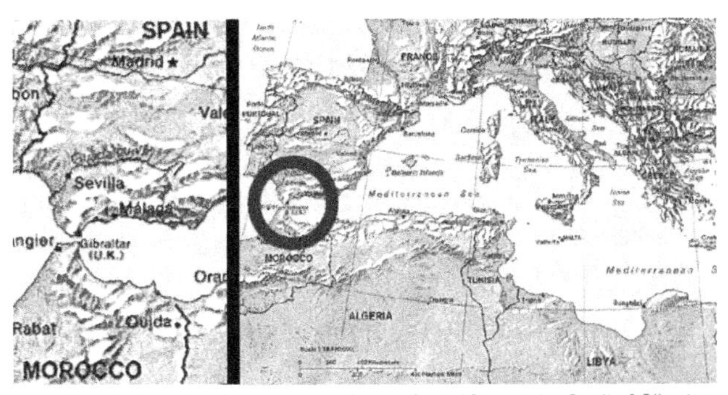

Less than 9 miles of ocean separates Europe from Africa at the Strait of Gibraltar

Knowing the value of seaports like the Suez Canal and the **Strait of Gibraltar**, Adolf Hitler wanted to secure the region with his own troops.

It was obvious that Italian military power in North Africa had begun to crumble.

With the British on the offensive, Italy was losing control of the area quickly. Key battles in East Africa had caused the less prepared Italians to lose ground. Large numbers of Italian soldiers were surrendering or dying, and Germany was forced to change the plans.

The invasion of England had become too costly for Hitler. With more losses than they planned, the Luftwaffe and the navy had to redirect some of their effort to defend Africa.

Define
ARSENAL

A collection of different weapons of war

From the icy waters of the North Atlantic to the jungles of Southeast Asia to the barren sands of the Sahara Desert, World War 2 was expanding.

The United States began setting aside huge amounts of money for the **arsenal** needed if war came to the west.

All of the nations across the world were spending a majority of their budgets on weapons and supplies.

ABOVE: A factory worker in Canada making helmets for soldiers. RIGHT: Many workers were women as the men were off fighting the war.

Deep inside of Europe far behind enemy lines, millions of average citizens were fighting a very different war. They became the victims of Nazi war crimes that would shock the entire world.

Countless wedding rings taken from Jewish victims of the Holocaust

Jewish civilians faced an enemy that would threaten the very survival of their race. Before the end of the war in 1945, Nazi Germany would kill two thirds of the entire Jewish population of Central

Europe. Millions of people were targeted for murder or imprisonment simply because they were Jewish.

The mass murder of Jews is called the "Holocaust" which is two Greek words, meaning "whole" and "burnt," because many of the bodies of Jewish victims were burnt after they died.

Many died of either starvation or disease, or were shot. Countless others were also killed by poisonous gas. The crimes against people who were not even soldiers were unequaled in the history of the world.

Keeping the Nazi arsenal strong was a huge mission. Hitler and the German leaders knew that slave labor could help keep the war effort supplied.

As the Nazi war factories began to be targeted by British bombers, the Germans pushed their prisoners even harder.

Prisoners were forced to work long hours without food or sleep

Nazi "concentration camps" were prisons where Jewish civilians and prisoners of war were forced to work long hours without food or sleep.

Bodies of Holocaust death camp victims

Living conditions at the prisons were very bad. When prisoners were unable to work, they were killed.

"We were not slaves; our status was much lower. We were like a piece of sandpaper which, rubbed once or twice, becomes useless and is thrown away to be burned with the waste". - Tad Goldsztajn, Holocaust survivor

"The Final Solution"

Adolf Hitler would later order the murder of all Jewish people in Europe. The Nazis called this policy "the final solution of the Jewish problem".

An estimated 6 million people of Jewish ancestry were killed in the Holocaust, including 3 million men, 2 million women, and 1 million children.

Christians and people with birth defects, including babies, were exterminated as well.

The Nazi poster below reads: "60,000 Reichsmarks: this is what this person suffering from (birth) defects costs the Community of Germans during his lifetime. Fellow Citizen, that is your money, too". The suggestion is that some people don't deserve to live.

The Nazis tried to hide the existence of death camps from the rest of the world because they knew it would make their enemies fight harder. Terrible crimes against innocent civilians also happened on the other side of the world as well.

For six weeks in 1937, Japanese troops brutally murdered an estimated 250,000 to 300,000 civilians and unarmed soldiers. Many were killed in cruel ways such as beheading. It was called the **Nanking Massacre**.

Of all the horrible tragedies of World War 2, the murder of helpless unarmed people will always be remembered as the worst.

After the war, many military leaders were found guilty and executed for their part in crimes against humanity.

Barbarossa

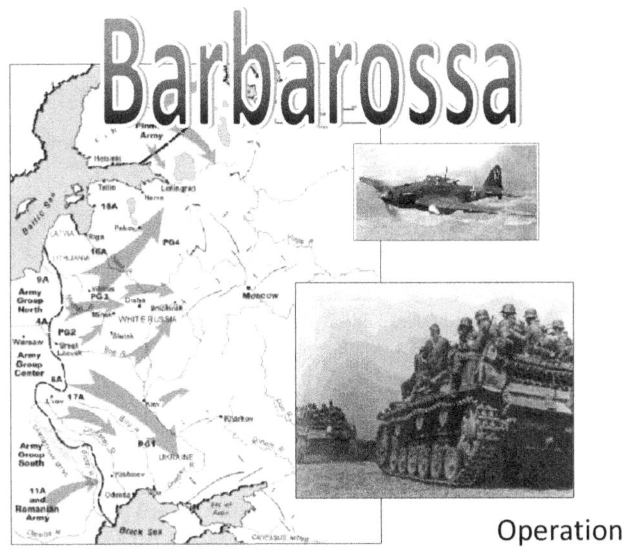

Operation Barbarossa was the code name for a massive invasion of the Soviet Union by Nazi Germany. It began in the spring of 1941 but was planned much earlier.

> Define
> ***IDEOLOGY***
> A belief system that shapes thoughts and action

Adolf Hitler had first hinted at going to war with Soviet Russia as early as 1925 in his book *"Mein Kampf"* (German for "My Struggle").

Nazi **ideology** was based on a belief that they were better than other people. Because they were white, for one thing, Nazis thought they were superior. Hitler also promoted a policy of *Lebensraum*, German for "living room".

Hitler's idea of more "living room" meant that Germany would need to expand its borders. Nazis believed they deserved to own the territory that belonged to races he considered inferior.

This policy meant that Germans should take what they wanted, even if it meant having to relocate other people and commit *genocide* (mass murder).

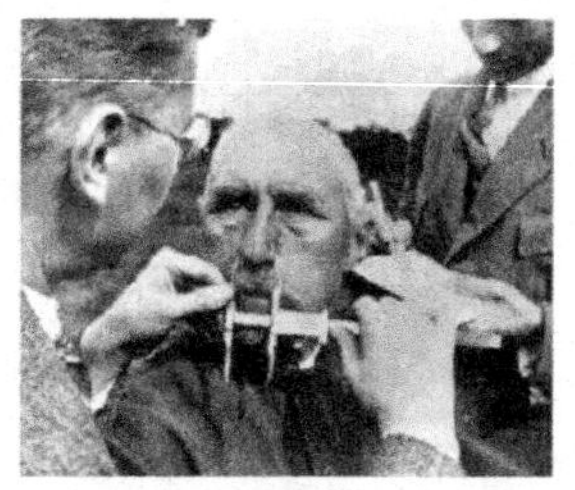

Nazi inspectors examine a man to determine his race

Lebensraum also caused the Nazis to think it was okay to force others into slave labor. Hitler viewed the invasion of the Soviet Union as a way to meet four major goals:

Nazi Goals of Operation Barbarossa

1. To gain fuel from Russian oil fields
2. To capture valuable farmland
3. To force Soviets into slavery
4. To seize more "living room"

Before the invasion, Germany and Russia had signed a nonaggression agreement, to keep peace between them. Both governments were a lot alike.

The Soviet Union, for example, also had concentration camps like the Nazis where millions were put to death.

And dictators who ruled with an iron fist controlled both nations. Still, there was deep suspicion, and neither side trusted the other. The hatred between communists and Nazis was deep rooted.

In the early years after World War One, the two political parties had clashed. Hitler learned to hate the communists as they competed for power in Germany.

Propaganda posters were used to inspire the Russian people

Joseph Stalin, the Soviet dictator, was aware of Hitler's dislike of communists and the people of the Soviet Union.

All the same, Stalin did not want war with Germany. Stalin's plan was to build up his military forces secretly. When and if war came to Russia, he wanted to be ready.

With more than 25,000 tanks and 20,000 airplanes, the Soviet Union a-massed a huge army of over five million soldiers and was totally equipped for war. The problem was unproven leaders and false information about German combat strategies.

By the summer of 1941, Germany had mastered the **Blitzkrieg** (lightning war). Despite all their planning, the Soviet Union was about to be caught unprepared.

Nazi forces gearing for a massive invasion of the Soviet Union, June 1941

Largest Invasion ever Assembled

As Germany prepared for the largest military invasion in history, Hitler's top leaders were not all in agreement.

Some thought the plan was too complex or too early. Many Nazi generals did not like the idea of opening an "**eastern front**" until the Battle of Britain was decided. But despite the opposition from his top counselors, Hitler insisted Operation Barbarossa be carried out.

In the early hours of June 22nd, 1941, the largest invasion force ever assembled began the attack against the Soviets.

Emboldened by the strength of over 4 million men, 600,000 motorized vehicles, 4,300 aircraft, and 750,000 horses, the Nazi blitzkrieg stormed east.

Emperor Frederick Barbarossa of Germany

The mission to invade Russia was named after **Frederick Barbarossa**, a German ruler who was crowned king of Germany in the year 1152. He would later become emperor of the Holy Roman Empire and lead the third Crusade to capture Jerusalem from the Muslims. Hitler chose the name because of Barbarossa's ambition and the fact that his enemies feared him so much.

The invasion broke treaties with Russia and would eventually cause tens of millions of deaths on both sides.

Along with the German army and air force, the invasion also included Italians, Romanians, Hungarian, and Finnish soldiers.

Every man, woman, and child along the Russian front would be involved in defending the Soviet homeland.

Axis forces led by Nazi Germany invade Russia along a front 1800 miles wide

The German attack was spread along an *1800-mile wide front*, about the length of the border between the United States and Mexico.

Despite all their preparations, the Soviet army was simply overwhelmed with the force, size, and speed of the Nazi invasion over such a vast area.

The original goal of the mission was to capture land beyond the Soviet capital of Moscow on what was called the **A-A line.** This line connected the cities of Arkhangelsk in the north and Astrakhan in the south on the Caspian Sea.

Hitler's plan depended on his immense army reaching the A-A line before the harsh Russian winter. The imaginary line divides the Soviet Union at the Asian and European border.

At first, Operation Barbarossa was a huge victory for the Nazis. Three million Russian soldiers were taken prisoner.

Although the Russians had far more tanks and planes than the Germans, much of their equipment was outdated and the leaders lacked a clear plan. Tanks ran out of gas as supplies lines were destroyed by the German's fast advance. Many Soviet airplanes were destroyed on the ground due to the surprise attack.

Most of the Russian prisoners died of starvation. Killing the Soviets, or letting prisoners die was part of the plan. Hitler wanted to get rid of them to make room for Germanic people to live in the land east of Poland.

German soldiers blitz the Soviet border east of Poland, June 1941

The mission may have succeeded if the Nazis had begun in the spring as planned, instead of later in the summer.

Three divisions of German troops forced their way deep into Soviet territory. The north and south army were met with strong resistance but still managed to break through.

As the conflict stretched into the fall, the Germans advanced toward their objective, but rain and mud stalled their progress.

Nazi mechanized unit bogged down in mud

Army Group Center tried desperately to capture Moscow, but the Soviets fought back with a larger force and more strength than Hitler had predicted. In early December, as winter set in, the Nazis forces reached within 5 miles of the Soviet capital. One general reported that he could see the spiral tops of the **Kremlin** (Russian for "fortress") in Moscow.

> Define
> ***KREMLIN***
> Spiral-topped fortress buildings in Russia

But it was too late. The severe Russian winter stopped the Germans in their tracks and they were stuck for another month. This gave the Soviet Red Army enough time to wait for more troops and supplies to arrive from the eastern Soviet Union.

Reinforcements arrived from eastern Soviet Union after the Germans were stalled

With the three Nazi divisions stretched too thin, most of the Nazi army didn't have enough supplies or proper clothing to survive the winter.

Many Germans were taken prisoner or died of exposure to the cold. What started as a terrible disaster for the Soviets turned out to be the beginning of the end of the **Third Reich**.

Some historians compare Hitler's failure to the Russian victory that destroyed Napoleon's army in the winter of 1812.

Painting depicting the defeat of Napoleon's army by Russia in the winter of 1812

Even though Germany kept trying to invade the Soviet Union, Hitler could never accomplish his goals.

Operation Barbarossa accounted for an astonishing 95% of all German deaths *in the entire war.*

As many as 20 million Russians lost their lives as the conflict between Germany and the Soviet Union dragged on. It lasted a total of four years until the Soviets pushed back all the way to the German capital of Berlin in 1945.

December 1941 marked a major turning point in World War 2. Germany's failed attempt to conquer the Soviet Union left the Nazi military weakened and the Soviets enraged with revenge to fight on the side of the allies. Hitler's army would never regain the strength it had before Barbarossa.

Another event that would change the course of the war was the surprise attack on the American naval base in Hawaii. The base was named **Pearl Harbor**. The date was December 7th, 1941.

The attack on Pearl Harbor brought America into the war without warning, leaving no doubt that things would never be the same.

In the early hours of a beautiful South Pacific Sunday morning, many American sailors were still sleeping. They had no way of knowing that the Empire of Japan had been planning a full-scale attack for several months. Six Japanese aircraft carriers carrying over 400 planes were sailing for the northern part of Oahu.

Relations between the United States and Japan had not been good for many years. As a safeguard, President Roosevelt decided to move the American Pacific naval fleet from San Diego, California to Pearl Harbor, Hawaii earlier in 1941.

RIGHT: American President Franklin D. Roosevelt

Define

PREEMPTIVE

Something done before others can take action

In order to conquer the oil rich territories of Southeast Asia, Japanese military planners believed that they had to launch a **preemptive** strike against the American Pacific fleet.

Relations between the United States and Japan had not been good for many years

With their Empire expanding in Asia and the western Pacific Ocean, Japan could not risk America standing in the way. Emperor Hirohito decided to gamble that the surprise attack would break the spirit of Americans.

But it actually had the opposite effect. The attack brought the nation together like never before. For the remainder of the war "Remember Pearl Harbor!" would be a rally cry for the United States.

On November 26, all six of Imperial Japan's aircraft carriers departed on the long journey across the western Pacific. Several other warships and submarines escorted the carriers in the largest attack fleet ever assembled.

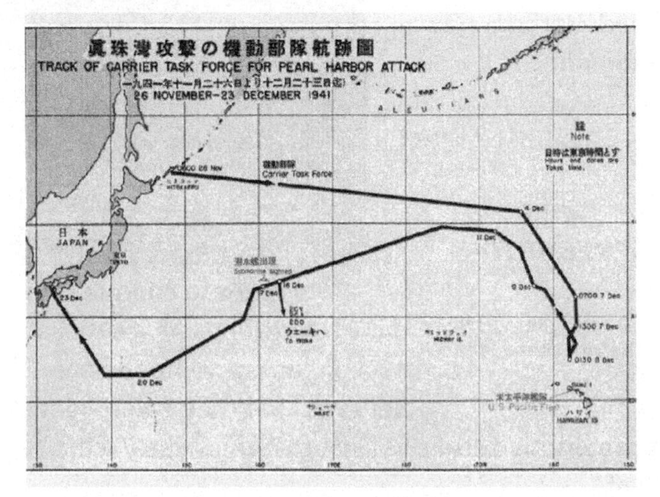

Japanese tracking map of the Pearl Harbor carrier task force

While darkness still masked the skies above the Hawaiian Islands, the first wave of warplanes bolted from the carriers.

The first wave of 183 planes (and soon after a second wave of 171 more) stormed the naval base and began a destructive air strike that would leave over 2,400 Americans dead. More than 1,200 were also wounded. It was the worst attack on America in history.

Japanese flagship aircraft carrier *Akagi* (Japanese: 赤城 "Red Castle")

The attack came as a complete shock to the American people. Most had believed that America would sooner or later go to war with Japan. But few thought the Japanese were capable of such a large-scale operation as the attack on Pearl Harbor.

As Americans were leaving church services in Washington DC on a typical Sunday afternoon, warplanes crowded the skies over the tropical paradise of Oahu.

Japanese fighters and dive-bombers rained destruction on the unsuspecting sailors and marines at the base in Pearl Harbor.

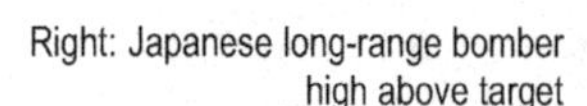

Right: Japanese long-range bomber high above target

The main targets of the mission were the battleships anchored in the shallower water of the harbor. Japan knew that attacking ships at anchor meant a less likelihood of sinking them, but they were determined to damage the battleships beyond repair.

Japanese military leaders, including Pearl Harbor task force commander Vice Admiral **Chūichi Nagumo**, shown to the right, were convinced that *battleships* would decide the war.

230 aircraft and eighteen ships were destroyed or damaged, including the battleship Arizona where 1,177 sailors and soldiers were killed. The Arizona accounted for nearly half of all American deaths.

Japanese leaders discussed a third wave attack, which Admiral Nagumo decided against. It would be a decision he would later regret.

The third wave would have targeted submarines and fuel tanks, as well as the intelligence command center.

Experts agree that the third wave would have actually set back the Pacific War for America more than the first two waves.

Since all 3 U.S. aircraft carriers were at sea in a training exercise, they were also spared.

World War 2 era American aircraft carrier

Aircraft carriers, along with submarines, and *not* battleships would be the main vessels the U.S. Navy would use against the Japanese.

Only 90 minutes later the attack on Pearl Harbor was over. The next day President Roosevelt addressed Congress and asked for a declaration of war against Japan.

Roosevelt called December 7th *"a date which will live in infamy"*.

After considering entering World War 2 for only one hour, Congress officially declared war on the Empire of Japan. Of the 471 senators and members of congress, only one, Jeannette Rankin, the first woman ever elected to Congress, voted against going to war. Most Americans favored the decision as well.

ABOVE: USS Arizona ablaze at Pearl Harbor.
LEFT: FDR signs declaration of war on Japan.

Roosevelt's signature three hours after the decision was merely a formality, as only Congress has power to declare war. But the image made a strong impact around the world.

Due in part to a promise made to the United States, Great Britain also declared war on Japan. Within days, Germany and Italy declared war on America, keeping with the Axis Powers' treaty.

As nations continued to choose sides, the entire planet smoldered in hostility. The war factories of every nation great and small were or soon would be in full production.

Within days of the attack on Pearl Harbor, Japan made bold moves in Far East Asia. Japanese forces continued their push into Malaya and invaded Thailand, the Philippines, and Burma.

Japanese paratroopers secure Sumatra and dominate Southeast Asia as 1941 comes to an end.

Operation Drumbeat

American tanker torpedoed by a German U-Boat off the Atlantic coast of the USA

After declaring war on the United States on December 11th 1941, Germany wasted no time. Within a week, a plan to attack freight ships off the eastern Atlantic coast of America was activated.

Nazi submarine crews departing for North American coastal waters

Due to the fact that the United States Navy did not have vessels or weapons suitable to prevent submarine attacks, German **U-Boats** were chosen to carry out the mission, codenamed Operation Drumbeat.

After Pearl Harbor, America feared a Japanese attack along the west coast of California. Naval officials were hesitant to redirect their limited resources to prevent German attacks in the Atlantic Ocean.

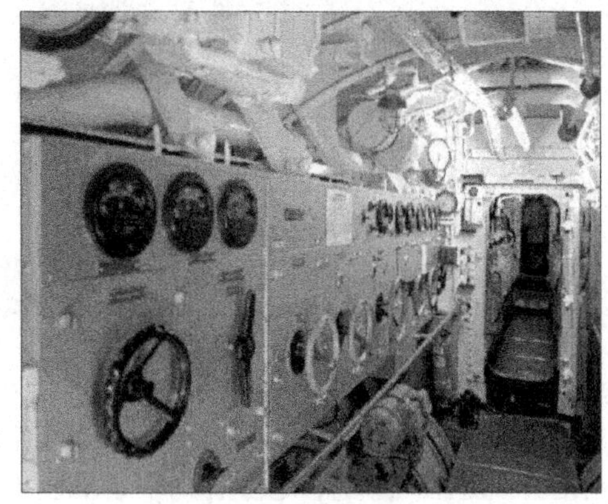

ABOVE: U-Boat engine room; BELOW: German Type VII submarine

Beginning in January 1942, German sub-marines patrolled the North American Atlantic coast from Maine to Florida mostly unchallenged. Nazi U-Boats even ventured into the Caribbean and the Gulf of Mexico.

When attacks became common at the mouth of the Mississippi River and the Panama Canal, the U.S. Navy had to act quickly.

German naval commanders called the attacks on merchant shipping "the American shooting season".

Cruising the eastern coastline of the United States by night, the German U-Boat strategy relied on identifying the outline of freight ships against the lights of cities such as New York, Miami, and New Orleans.

As a major part of the Battle of the Atlantic, Operation Drumbeat proved to be very successful, stretching as far south as Brazil.

Factors that ended Operation Drumbeat:

- The formation of Allied convoys to escort merchant shipping
- Development of anti-submarine weapons such as "depth charge" mines
- SONAR technology allowed the Allies to detect U-boats beneath the ocean surface
- English and American ability to break Germany's secret code

From January to August 1942, German and Italian submarines sank over *six hundred* oil tankers and other merchant ships in the western Atlantic and Caribbean. Only 22 Axis submarines were lost. One was sunk in the Gulf of Mexico just 45 miles south of the mouth of Mississippi River.

Define
SONAR
Undersea version of RADAR, which allows you to "hear" subs

Along with the use of **sonar**, British and American engineers worked to break the German secret code. In addition, convoy escorts and new anti-submarine weapons ended Nazi U-Boat *"wolf pack"* attacks on the Americas. For a while,

Churchill and the British military leaders thought the Nazis could win the Battle of the Atlantic.

The supply of oil and other materials from the United States and South America had all but stopped. Without the determined effort of the Allies, Hitler may have come one step closer to his dream of ruling the world.

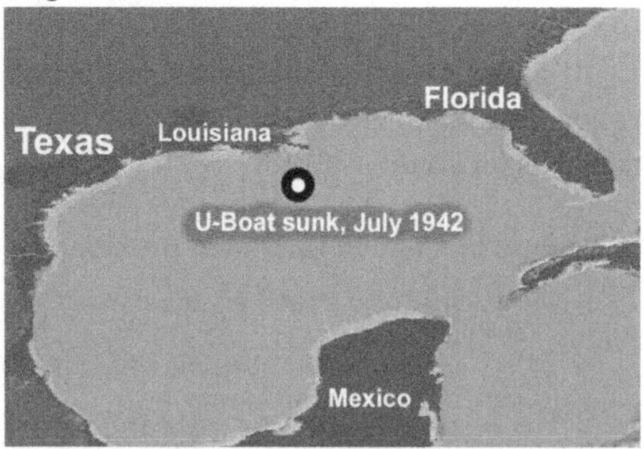

Location of sunken Nazi submarine U-166 off the coast of Louisiana

As the Germans struck a heavy blow to Allied merchant ships critical to the war effort in the Atlantic, the Japanese continue to expand their power in the Pacific. President Roosevelt gave the order for General **Douglas MacArthur** and his forces to evacuate the Philippines. MacArthur leaves, vowing to return.

General MacArthur, one of 4 five-star generals in US Army history

In April 1942, Japanese soldiers completed the capture of the Philippines and Bataan.

Filipino and American prisoners of war were forced to march 80 miles under horrible conditions, in what was called the "Bataan Death March". Many were beaten, murdered, or allowed to starve. Thousands of soldiers died before they reached the prison camp.

Guarded by Japanese soldiers, prisoners rest along the Bataan Death March

From he desert sand dunes of North Africa to the subtropical jungles of Burma to the Gulf coast of the American south, the entire world was erupting in violent warfare.

It seemed that nowhere on the planet was safe anymore.

As the United States geared for total war with the Axis powers, common citizens prepared to do their part. All across America, programs to help the war effort were begun. Everything that could help ensure victory in the war was rationed or restricted. Recycling was also necessary. From gasoline, paper, rubber, metals of all kinds, and even left-over cooking fat, Americans were doing their part on the "home front".

Much of the materials were recycled to produce weapons or equipment. Some items like silk stockings and rubber were recycled to make up for the lack of imports from Axis occupied parts of Asia. Even the U.S. government limited the use of metals like the copper in pennies. Except for a handful minted in copper by mistake, all of the 1943 pennies were made of steel. For this reason, genuine 1943 copper pennies are extremely rare and valuable, with only 40 known to exist, according to the U.S. Mint.

Tokyo Raid

B25 Mitchell bomber taking off the USS Hornet flight deck

In the weeks after the surprise attack on Pearl Harbor, Americans watched and listened for relief from their fear.

With Nazi submarine attacks threatening America's security in the Atlantic and anxiety over the situation in the Pacific, America needed a boost of confidence. The U.S. Army decided to make a bold move and bomb targets in Tokyo, Japan.

To carry out the plan, they chose Lt. Colonel **Jimmy Doolittle** to plan and lead the Tokyo Raid. The daring mission is also known as the *Doolittle Raid.*

The raid made history in many ways. It was the only operation of its kind before or since.

Originally planned by President Roosevelt just two weeks after the Pearl Harbor attack, the operation remained top secret even to the pilots. They had been asked to volunteer for an "extremely hazardous" mission.

After three weeks of intense training, and with limited instructions, the pilots and crewmembers, known as "the Doolittle Raiders," boarded the aircraft carrier *USS Hornet* in California.

Loaded with sixteen modified **B25 Mitchell bombers**, the Hornet sailed toward Japan. Along the way, they met up with another aircraft carrier, the USS Enterprise, and several escort ships.

Ten hours before the raid was to begin, a Japanese ship spotted the convoy. Losing the element of surprise, Doolittle decided to launch the B25s right away, knowing the planes wouldn't have enough fuel to return to the carrier.

All sixteen B25s were launched safely. The raiders approached major Japanese cities six hours later and began bombing military and industrial targets.

Although the Tokyo Raid did not cause major damage, it deeply affected the morale of the American people. After Pearl Harbor, the country needed a boost of confidence.

Define
PSYCHOLOGICAL
Something that makes you think differently or changes your mind

Another important result of the raid was the **psychological** effect, causing confusion and tension among the Japanese military leaders. The Japanese Navy was embarrassed for letting an enemy aircraft carrier convoy approach the homeland so close, and escape safely.

Columbus Evening Dispatch

OHIO'S GREATEST HOME DAILY

U.S. WARPLANES RAIN BOMBS ON LEADING CITIES OF JAP EMPIRE

YANK BOMBING PLANES CARRY WAR TO ENEMY

Tokyo, Yokohama, Kobe And Nagoya Hit in Big Three-Hour Offensive

HUNDREDS OF BUILDINGS REPORTED WRECKED IN RAID ON JAPS

United Nations On Offensive In Far Pacific

TRANSFER OF $2,000,000 TO AID DEFENSE SOUGHT

NAVY MAY TAKE OVER OPERATION OF AIRPORT

Late War Bulletins

At first, Colonel Jimmy Doolittle thought he would be in trouble due to the lack of major damage to Japanese targets and also because all 16 bombers were lost. But instead, he was awarded the **Medal of Honor** by President Roosevelt and later promoted to general for his courage and leadership.

Of the 80 airmen involved in the raid, 69 escaped alive, with barely enough fuel to crash land in China. Eight raiders were taken captive. Four died in captivity, 3 executed and one from disease.

American forces freed the other 4 prisoners in August 1945.

The Political Leaders of World War 2

Franklin D. Roosevelt, President of the United States
Sir Winston Churchill, Prime Minister of the United Kingdom
Chiang Kai-shek, Chairman of the National Government of China
Joseph Stalin, Premier of the Soviet Union
Charles De Gaulle, Prime Minister, French Provincial Government

Hirohito, Emperor of Japan
Adolf Hitler, Chancellor of Germany
Benito Mussolini, Head of Government of Italy

American Theatre

Alaskan area targeted by the small Japanese invasion force in 1942

The vast majority of fighting in World War 2 occurred in Europe, Asia, and North Africa. North and South America were mostly unaffected. This was mainly due to the distance across the Pacific and Atlantic Oceans.

United States Army Air Force Boeing B-17 long-range bomber

But the United States did experience minimal attacks from both Germany and Japan. As early as 1937, Adolf Hitler expressed his desire to strike America.

The Japanese had made plans to carry out raids on the west coast of the United States, as well as the **Panama Canal**, the major route between America's east and west coasts.

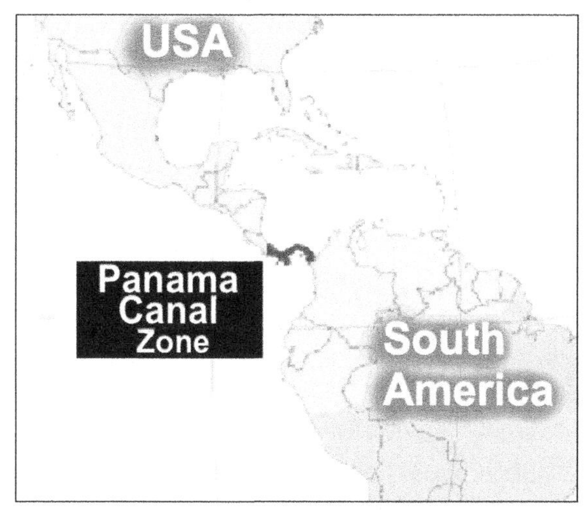

Germany and Japan were developing long-range bombers like the American Boeing B17 "Flying Fortress". The Nazis called their project "Amerika-Bomber".

Nazi Messerschmitt Me 264 Long Range Bomber

The Nazi Amerika-Bomber was designed to reach The U.S., a distance of about 3600 miles, but the problem was returning to Europe. Before it could reach mainland Europe it would need to refuel.

As the Japanese constructed a **prototype** of its own long-range bomber, military leaders discussed the idea of bombing strategic targets in the western United States. They would then meet up with German U-boats in the Gulf of Mexico to refuel.

Captured Japanese ZERO fighter plane after the Battle of Dutch Harbor

Both Axis powers would have to abandon their long-range bomber programs after suffering major losses in 1942. In view of Hitler's failed attack on the Soviet Union, Germany would not be able to mount an offensive against America.

Even though long-range bombing plans were unlikely, Japan still acted quickly to take advantage of the surprise attack on Pearl Harbor.

Continuing their plans to attack the United States, the Japanese made advances against the Aleutian Islands in Alaska.

In June of 1942 a convoy of Japanese ships, which included two light carriers, sailed for the American base at Dutch Harbor in the Alaska territory.

The plan was to secure the island rim in the Bering Sea and protect northern Japan from a possible attack by the United States.

Following an air raid over the Alaskan territory of Dutch Harbor, Japanese troops landed on the islands of Attu and Kiska.

Japanese forces occupied the islands for almost a year until a bloody battle with American troops forced them to abandon the region. It was the only time American and Japanese troops engaged in freezing Arctic weather.

Although no major damage was ever done on American soil, other attempts were made by the Japanese to cause turmoil and fear against Americans.

Japanese submarine-based bomber

Japanese submarines fired shells at an oilfield off the coast of California near Santa Barbara and, in the only attack on a mainland military installation, at

Fort Stevens in Oregon. Neither resulted in loss of lives, but did cause panic along the west coast of the U.S.

North American citizens and officials were constantly on the alert, watching for attacks on the coastline from Mexico to Canada. Military bases were reinforced with more troops and equipment and protected by barbed wire.

Other attempts to terrorize the people of America and Canada late in the war resulted in the Japanese Navy releasing thousands of "balloon bombs," some of which drifted as far east as Michigan, with one killing five children and a woman in Oregon.

RIGHT: The owner of this Japanese-American owned store, a graduate of the University of California, was forced to close and relocate to a Detainee Camp

In one of the most controversial decisions of World War 2, the American government officially detained over 100,000 Japanese-Americans for fear that some might be spies or take the side of the enemy.

The detainees were sent to "War Relocation Camps" authorized by the U.S. Government where most would stay for the remainder of the war.

Signed into law by President Roosevelt, the decision to detain Japanese-Americans was eventually ruled illegal by the Supreme Court.

In 1945, near the end of the war, detainees were free to leave.

American family of Japanese descent prepares to evacuate.

Over forty years later, American President Ronald Reagan signed a bill passed by Congress officially apologizing for the treatment of detainees during World War 2.

Ironically, the most decorated soldiers in the history of the United States Army were the members of *442nd Infantry Regiment*, consisting almost entirely of Japanese-Americans. They fought mostly in Europe against the Nazis, earning the esteemed nickname the "Purple Heart Battalion" due to their combat performance.

In 1942, the war developed at a rapid pace. The eastern front in Europe saw intense action as the Soviet army repelled the Nazis at **Stalingrad**. Close combat from house to house resulted in the bloodiest battle in world history.

The Battle of Stalingrad was the deadliest in history

Japanese and American aircraft carriers faced off for the first time at the **Battle of the Coral Sea** near Australia.

One American fleet carrier and one Japanese light carrier were sunk.

U.S. aircraft carrier Lexington in flames just before sinking at the Battle of the Coral Sea

In the deserts of Egypt, Rommel's Afrika Corps succeeded in stopping British tanks from advancing. And a 1942 naval battle at the island of Midway in the Pacific would be a critical turning point in the war.

ABOVE: Mitsubishi A6M2 Zero fighters preparing to launch from Japanese carrier Akagi, BELOW: *Left*, five-star Admiral Chester W. Nimitz, commander-in-chief United States Navy Pacific fleet. *Right*, Admiral Isoroku Yamamoto, commander-in-chief of the Imperial Japanese Navy

The historic **Battle of Midway** began the same day as the Aleutian Island Campaign, but was on a much greater scale. The Japanese objective was to destroy the remaining American carrier fleet and occupy Midway Island.

Knowing the risk of confronting the enemy on such a magnitude would mean great gains in the Pacific war, both nations committed large armadas to the battle.

USS Yorktown after being hit by a Japanese dive-bomber, Battle of Midway

The Element of Surprise

Even though the Japanese had the advantage of a larger fleet, they lost the element of surprise. Unlike the attack on Pearl Harbor, the United States was aware of Japan's intentions at Midway. They had cracked the Imperial Japanese Navy's code.

With an impressive force of 4 aircraft carriers, 2 battleships, several support ships, and nearly 250 carrier-based airplanes, the Japanese fleet approached Midway Island on June 4th, 1942.

Mistakenly believing the flotilla had arrived undetected, Admiral Isoroku Yamamoto, commander-in-chief of the Imperial Japanese Navy, proceeded with the complex plan.

American scout planes spotted the Japanese strike force and relayed the information to the U.S. high command.

Admiral Chester W. Nimitz, commander-in-chief United States Navy Pacific fleet, had cobbled together a fleet of three carriers including **Yorktown**, which the Japanese believed they had sunk in the Coral Sea one month earlier.

TOP LEFT: US Navy Devastators unfold their wings prior to take off from USS Enterprise
ABOVE: U.S. Navy Douglas SBD-3 “Dauntless” bomber launches from USS Hornet

After a series of **reconnaissance** flights and failed bombing raids, aircraft from the U.S. Navy, Marines, and Army Air Corps finally succeeded in sinking all four Japanese carriers.

Define
RECONNAISSANCE
A method to secretly gather information, especially about an enemy

The **Yorktown** was the only American carrier sunk. Ten times as many Japanese lives as Americans were lost, over 3,000 in all. And all of the Japanese planes were destroyed.

It was a clear victory for the United States. For the first time, the Empire of Japan had lost a major battle at sea, perhaps the most important battle of the entire Pacific War. Although the Japanese navy remained a powerful force in the Pacific until the end of the war, it never regained superiority over America.

After the Battle of Midway, the Empire of Japan's area of control was gradually reduced by the growing American supremacy in the Western Pacific region.

With advances in aircraft technology, the Battle of Midway proved that the age of battleship warfare was over. No longer would ships alone decide conflicts at sea. Four Japanese carriers were destroyed not by other warships, but by bombardment from the sky.

This left the Japanese Navy with only two fleet carriers, both of which were undergoing repairs in Japan.

With the victory at Midway, American morale was high again. Even though the attack on Pearl

Harbor occurred only six months earlier, Midway brought a sense of relief and hope to Americans.

Hirohito and his military advisers never discovered the truth that their secret code had been deciphered. Throughout the rest of the war, they continued to use the same code. The Japanese people were not told of the devastating defeat. Instead, the government announced the battle as a victory for Japan.

LEFT: General George S. Patton; RIGHT: American troops aboard an armored amphibious personnel carrier prior to storming the beach in Algiers, November 1942

The first major American combat action in the war against the Nazis began in late 1942 in Northern Africa. Operation Torch was a bold plan to storm the beaches of Northern Africa that French troops loyal to Hitler were assigned to defend.

The mission was a joint Allied effort to free the southern Mediterranean coast from the grip of the Axis powers.

British tank commander Lt. General **Bernard Montgomery** (above) succeeded at striking back at Rommel, but the Allies needed to clear the Germans completely out of Africa to establish a base for invading Europe.

Along the southern coast of the Mediterranean, Montgomery would advance from the east. American forces, under the command of General **Dwight D. Eisenhower**, would push toward Tunisia from the west, trapping the Germans in between.

RIGHT: Allied commander American General Dwight D. Eisenhower

A key part of the plan involved the "Vichy French" and their allegiance to the Nazis. Hitler had promised he would not to occupy southern France.

But the promise was based on the condition that the Frenchmen remain loyal to the Nazi cause. American and British strategists were hoping the French would see the opportunity as a way to rejoin the Allies.

Once ashore however, some of the French soldiers remained loyal to their commander and resisted the American invasion before finally surrendering. Other Frenchmen welcomed the Allied invasion and did not resist.

After the Vichy French surrendered in Algiers and other beach cities in Morocco and Algeria, Hitler violated his agreement and invaded southern France.

Vichy France "Free Zone" was really a puppet state for Nazi Germany

In turn, the French military in Africa united with the Allies and fought against the Germans. With the Americans on the African continent, Hitler was surrounded by enemies.

But the fight was far from over. In fact, the first full scale clash between the Americans and Germans at the **Battle of the Kasserine Pass** was a disaster. The battle-hardened Nazis, who were more disciplined and better equipped, soundly defeated the American forces.

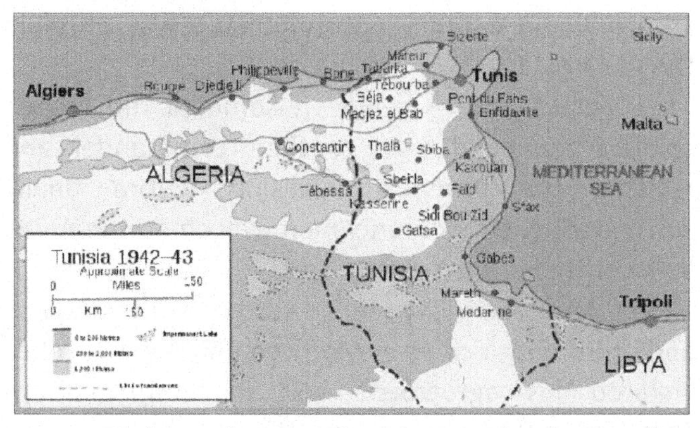

Pushing the American troops back 50 miles, Rommel's victory resulted in Eisenhower giving the American command to General **George S. Patton**.

Patton's aggressive methods proved to be what was needed to shape up his men quickly, earning him the nickname "Old blood and guts".

Ultimately the Allied forces wrestled the German and Italian resistance into retreat.

LEFT: General Patton encouraging his troops, Algeria 1942

Surrounded by the British and Americans, Axis troops finally surrendered in Tunisia in May of 1943. The Allies were now in control of the southern Mediterranean coast, poised for an attack on mainland Europe.

Allied command saw their best hope in Sicily, a plan that would repel the Italians and Germans, forcing them to retreat up the "boot" of Italy.

Tank Warfare North Africa

Tank Warfare North Africa

As 1942 came to a close, the Allies looked forward to the New Year with hope. For the first time, Japan was on the defensive as they retreated from major conflicts like the Battle of Guadalcanal.

LEFT: U.S. Marines storm the beach at Guadalcanal

In Eastern Europe, the Soviets pushed German forces back, resulting in major Nazi losses. And even though Rommel continued to resist the British and American squeeze from both sides, the Axis Powers had all but lost their command of Northern Africa.

By the early spring of 1943, the Nazis had abandoned their hope of retaining the southern Mediterranean coast. The plan to launch an attack against mainland Europe would soon become a reality.

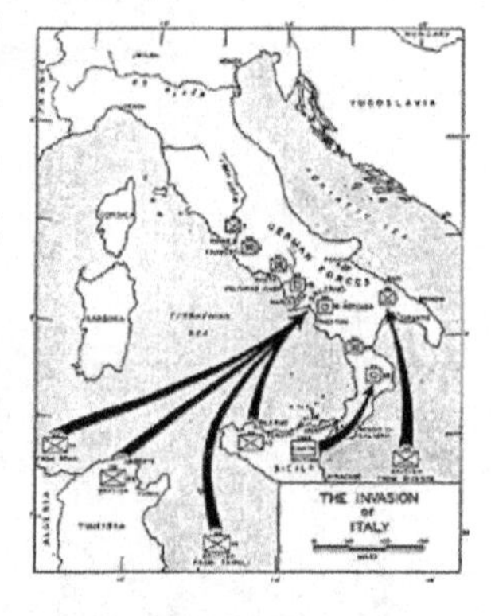

On July 9th, the Allied invasion of Sicily began with intense aerial and naval bombardment.

American task forces under General Patton, as well as British and Canadian troops would follow with a ground assault. Not ready to relinquish control, German paratroopers reinforced the Italians and Nazi troops already occupying the island.

By mid-August, however, the German high command realized their chance of winning the Sicilian Campaign was futile and ordered a retreat.

Italian Campaign

A U.S. Army medic attends a wounded American soldier in Sicily, August 9th, 1943

Even though the Allied leaders disagreed on the strategy of attack, the invasion of mainland Europe was sure to come. In the autumn of 1943, the Allied command commenced the attack.

For several months before the North Africa Campaign ended, Roosevelt and Churchill had debated on where the invasion of Europe should take place.

The American leaders insisted on a massive assault on Northern France while their British counterparts believed continued naval attacks in the Mediterranean would be more effective.

President Roosevelt eventually favored the British idea, with an agreement to attack Italy. Taking the Italians out of the war would weaken the Axis bond and force the Germans to redirect troops from the eastern front, allowing the Soviets to strengthen their effort in the east. As Allied planners prepared to launch the invasion, they were confident of minimal opposition from the Nazis, enabling a quick defeat of the Italian forces.

Nearly 30 nations signed the United Nations agreement to stand against the Nazis and Fascists in Europe and the Japanese Empire in Asia. Officially founded in June 1945, the alliance would eventually grow to become the organization it is known today, consisting of 193 member states with unprecedented power and influence.

The U.S. Army leadership was convinced that naval and aerial attacks would compromise a surprise attack. Choosing to send troops ashore at Salerno on the western coast without bombing proved a mistake, however, as the Allies met heavy resistance from the powerful German defensive force.

Led by General Montgomery, British forces landed on the beaches of Calabria at the "toe" of Italy on September 3rd.

Planned as a diversion from the main landing at Salerno, Montgomery met practically no opposition. The Germans did not fall for the scheme and had long retreated.

Soon after the invasion of their nation, the Italian government chose to surrender. The Allied plan seemed to be taking shape.

Benito Mussolini, who had been imprisoned since July by his own government after the Allied invasion of Sicily, was freed by German special forces on September 12th.

Mussolini formed a new government in northern Italy, the "Italian Social Republic". Many Italians in the north took up arms and fought against Mussolini and the Nazis.

The Tuskegee Airmen were the first all African-American fighter squadron pilots in United States aviation history. Although the American military was segregated during the war and black pilots endured racial discrimination, the Airmen proved their skillfulness and patriotism, first demonstrated in the Invasion of Sicily and the Italian Campaign

Southern Italy quickly responded to the Allies by assuming a "liberated" state, joining the fight against the Nazis. During this chaotic period, Italy was in a state of civil war and the Germans forcibly disarmed and imprisoned Italian troops and began detaining Italian Jews. Many Italians were killed.

Even without the support of Italian forces in the south, the Allies were met with fierce German resistance as they pushed north.

British forces launched the invasion on the "toe" of Italy at Calabria, as Americans embarked on the second phase of the invasion at Salerno.

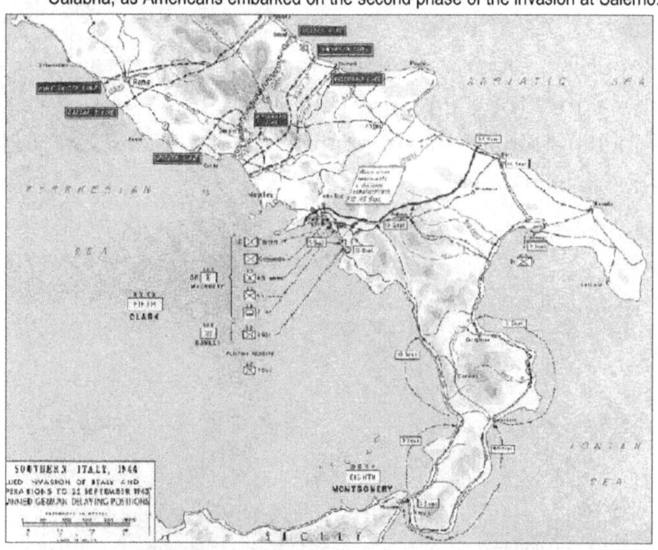

Convinced of an easy victory, Winston Churchill had declared that Italy was the "soft underbelly" of Europe. But the rough terrain of Italy's mountainous spine made it extremely difficult for the Allies.

German defensive fortification all but stalled the Allied troops from advancing. Hitler insisted on stopping the Allied advance at any cost.

As the American and British forces fought virtually uphill through the mountains of Italy, the Nazis quickly captured Rome, preparing for the Allied assault.

American soldiers launching a bazooka attack against a Nazi machine gun nest, Italian Campaign 1943

German troops fought back, stubbornly defending the continent as Hitler had commanded.

Germany now had guns pointing in practically every direction with losses growing everyday. The spread of Nazi tyranny had stopped and was now reversing.

Hitler demanded more of his troops than ever before. The **Wehrmacht** (German for "defense force," the official title of the combined Nazi military) was stretched beyond the limits of endurance. It was only a matter of time before Germany was broken. But the fight would rage on for two more years.

The Italian Campaign proved to be slow and costly. Only after the massive Allied invasion of France in June 1944 called D-Day would the German defenses in Italy be shattered.

Yakovlev Yak-3, Soviet Union

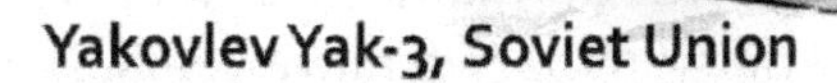

World War Two

"KEEP 'EM FLYING"

IS OUR BATTLE CRY!

FIRST CLASS FIGHTING MEN NEEDED

AVIATION CADETS . . . . . Young Men, 18 to 26 Years of Age Inclusive, for Air Crew Training as Bombardiers, Navigators and Pilots.

SOLDIERS . . . . Aggressive, Alert, Patriotic, Young Men, 18 and 19 Years of Age, Who Want to Fight for Their Country, Especially Desired.

APPLY TODAY AT ANY U. S. ARMY RECRUITING STATION

North American P-51 Mustang, USA

Strange Facts about World War 2

- The first naval battle of the war occurred off the coast of South America
- Adolf Hitler's nephew served in the U.S. Navy
- Nearly 30 years after Japan surrendered, a Japanese soldier came out of a Pacific jungle unaware that the war was over
- Lt. General Lesley McNair, the highest-ranking American soldier killed in WW2, was accidentally killed by a U.S. Army Air Corps bomb
- A faulty toilet sank German submarine U-120

Feuersturm

Never before World War 2, or since then for that matter, were airplanes used so extensively and in so many different ways. Heroic pilots slugged it out over the English Channel in legendary fighter planes like the RAF Hawker Hurricane and the Luftwaffe's Messerschmitt Bf 109.

The Japanese A6M "Zero" became the terror of the South Pacific skies in daring raids like the attack on Pearl Harbor. Numerous American bombers such as the B-17 "Flying Fortress" and the B-26 Marauder were famous for their contributions to the war.

American light bombers Douglas A-20 Invader and Mitchell B-26 Marauder

BELOW: Orville Wright flies the Wright Brothers' aeroplane in Ohio, November 1904

By 1943, aircraft design and production had evolved at a phenomenal pace since the **Wright Brothers** first flew a manned airplane forty years earlier.

Less than 220,000 airplanes were built during the entire five years of World War 1. By the end of the Second World War, over 300,000 airplanes were manufactured by the United States alone, with nearly 800,000 worldwide.

Aerial bombing had brought unimaginable destruction to cities over Europe and Asia early in the war. But by the summer of 1943, no one could have predicted the devastation that would soon rain down on Germany.

British planners, led by Winston Churchill, calculated the results of "precision bombing" that aimed to destroy only military and industrial targets with minimal civilian casualties.

British Wellington bombers targeting German factories

Pinpointing targets heavily defended by anti-aircraft artillery deep in German territory resulted in significant losses of RAF pilots and aircraft. This caused the British to reconsider their strategy. Their conclusion was less than desirable to the Americans.

As American and British air forces joined together for the first time in 1943, American leaders had yet to learn what the British had found out the hard way. The price of precision bombing was more than they could afford.

Agreeing to a compromise, the Allies planned a massive aerial attack code-named **Operation Gomorrah** on Hamburg, Germany. Chosen for its numerous military and industrial factories, Hamburg was also a port city, relatively close to Britain.

The plan called for the British to bomb the city by night followed by the Americans with precision daylight bombing. Both Churchill and Roosevelt agreed to the mission, knowing that many civilians would be killed.

German workers clearing rubble after heavy Allied attacks on Hamburg, July 1943

Counting on the German people to rise up against such destruction and overthrow Hitler's government, Allied commanders believed the risk would be worth taking if it ended the war quickly.

Throughout April and May, Hamburg was bombed extensively. With an enormous force never before assembled, the mission began in earnest in late July with nearly 800 British aircraft striking the city almost every night for a week.

The American daylight raids were all but suspended due to lack of daytime visibility caused by billowing smoke.

Just before midnight on July 27th, 1943, the British unleashed a fury so intense that it caused a firestorm unlike the world had ever seen before.

Lasting about three hours, the **Feuersturm** (German for firestorm) caused tornado-like winds up to 150 mph reaching temperatures of 1,500° F. The inferno caused asphalt streets to burst into flames and destroyed 16,000 multi-level apartment buildings, killing 30,000 people.

Both the Axis and Allied forces continued to concentrate on bombing factories and military installations until the end of the war, but targets populated by civilians were also hit, often intentionally, resulting in many deaths.

The Hamburg Feuersturm, and attacks on other cities like Berlin, London, Rome, and Tokyo, and especially the use of atomic bombs on Japan, have long been disputed as cruel and needless.

Neither side achieved their goal of breaking the enemy's morale. But many argue that the practice of targeting civilians was necessary to stop the efforts of Nazi Germany and Japan. Still, it remains one of the most tragic episodes of World War 2.

British children left homeless following the "London Blitz" by the Nazis

Time Line 1943

Tehran Conference, Allied leaders, including President Roosevelt, Prime Minister Churchill, and Soviet Premier Stalin meet to discuss war strategy

The Battle of Stalingrad comes to an end as German troops surrender to the Soviets

Japanese forces evacuate Guadalcanal, giving the Americans their first major ground victory in the Pacific War

As Allied troops pressed German and Japanese forces into retreat, American, British, and Soviet commanders met to plan the final push.

With the Nazis squarely on the defensive, Hitler's dream of world domination deteriorated more each passing month.

The superior strength of the Allies— and lack of trained personnel and fuel— had virtually put the once mighty Luftwaffe and **Kriegsmarine** (German for War Navy) out of commission by mid 1944.

In the Pacific, the Imperial Japanese Navy was also losing the war. Fighting for an improbable recovery of its former power and strength, the Japanese surrendered occupied territory and retreated.

The Allied fighting spirit caught the Japanese off guard. Rapid progress in American technology and production capability forced Japan to abandon the quest for control of Asia and resort instead to a defensive posture.

Indian and British forces turned the tide of the Japanese advance at the **Battle of Kohima**, forcing them to retreat at the border of India back into Burma. United States Marines captured key islands in the Pacific, routing the overwhelmed Japanese military forces. The Japanese would never regain the offensive.

Sikh colonists defend India from the Japanese at the Battle of Kohima, referred to as "the Stalingrad of the east," 1944

The Japanese people were taught that is was better to die with dignity than to surrender. Vowing to fight to the end, military leaders trained women and children in self-defense throughout the nation. In Nazi Germany, leaders of the Third Reich continued to persuade children to follow the Fuhrer.

Early in the Nazi movement, Adolf Hitler realized the importance of recruiting children

In 1922, early in the Nazi movement, Hitler began developing a military style program for German children, the **Hitlerjugend** (Hitler Youth). Many of the boys in the program would later become soldiers in the war.

In both Germany and Japan, citizens prepared for the looming Allied invasion. Hitler fortified the northern coast of France for the expected American and British offensive and Japanese military officials withdrew their troops

from South Pacific island territories after intense combat with Allied forces.

As the American Navy and Marines moved closer to mainland Japan, Roosevelt and his commanders calculated the cost of winning the war.

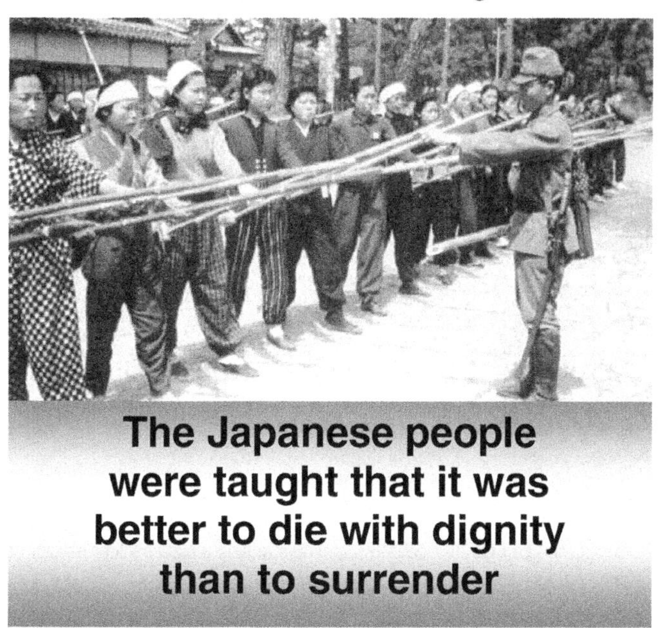

The Japanese people were taught that it was better to die with dignity than to surrender

Top American generals and admirals believed the final push in the Pacific War would mean massive casualties on both sides.

Manhattan Project

Under the veil of secrecy, a powerful new weapon was being designed that could end the war. American scientists, including German immigrants, were among the elite team of specialists working on a top-secret project called the "**Manhattan Project**".

First introduced in 1939 as a proposal supported by leading scientists including Albert Einstein, the Manhattan Project was given high-level approval by President Roosevelt almost immediately. The proposal warned of the development of *"extremely powerful bombs of a new type"* and recommended the United States take the lead in research and production of the new bombs.

By late 1944, the ambitious project had employed thousands of people at numerous sites and was close to developing the world's first atomic bomb.

LEFT: Albert Einstein with J. Robert Oppenheimer, who is often called the "father of the atomic bomb". BELOW: Allied personnel dismantling a Nazi nuclear reactor in Germany.

Fearing that Nazi Germany would win the atomic race, the American government needed to keep the project top secret.

Define
SABOTAGE
Activities aimed to slow, stop, or destroy an enemy's plans or projects

German scientists and engineers were indeed developing atomic weapons, and Allied forces **sabotaged** German laboratories and factories known to be a threat.

By the end of the war in 1945, the quest to successfully develop and use atomic weapons became an international race. Japan lagged behind due to a lack of resources. Soviet spies had gained access to the Manhattan Project and the Nazis were rumored to have actually tested an atomic bomb.

German submarine U-234, carrying weapons grade uranium oxide bound for Japan, surrendering to the U.S. Navy

What is known for certain is that after Germany's surrender in May 1945, **Nazi submarine U-234** was captured en route to Japan. Included in the cargo was 1200 pounds of uranium oxide, material needed to make an atomic bomb. This information was classified for decades and only recently released to the public.

With the dawn of the atomic age, weapons capable of destroying the planet became a reality. But the United States government leaders risked the consequences in order to end the war the quickest way possible.

The complex nature of a world war involving so many governments meant that trust, even among the Allies, was often hard to achieve. Because of different political and moral beliefs, the Allied partnership between the U.S. and the Soviet Union was shaky during the war. With the end of the war in sight, American and Soviet officials began planning how German territory, scientists, and technology would be divided.

But the Axis Powers weren't ready to give up. By the summer of 1944, Hitler had increased his efforts to deny the Allies an easy victory. Likewise, the Japanese high command was ready to defend their homeland at any cost.

Two critical strategies that the Axis Powers used toward the end of the war were somewhat successful at slowing the Allied advances.

One was the Japanese **Kamikaze** (Japanese for "divine wind") attacks against American ships, especially carriers.

ABOVE: Japanese Kamikaze attack on the USS Bunker Hill. LEFT: Japanese high school girls cheer a pilot as he takes off on a suicide mission.

After suffering major losses in the Pacific War and realizing the lack of adequate industrial capabilities, Japan resorted to training pilots for suicide missions.

Kamikaze pilots were trained to intentionally fly their planes into American ships. They were taught that to die for the Empire this way was a great honor. Pilots began training for kamikaze missions in June 1944 and they were carried out until the end of the war.

Another strategy used by the Axis was a milestone in technology. German scientists developed the first man-made object to ever fly into outer space, the **V-2 rocket**, shown below in an English diagram.

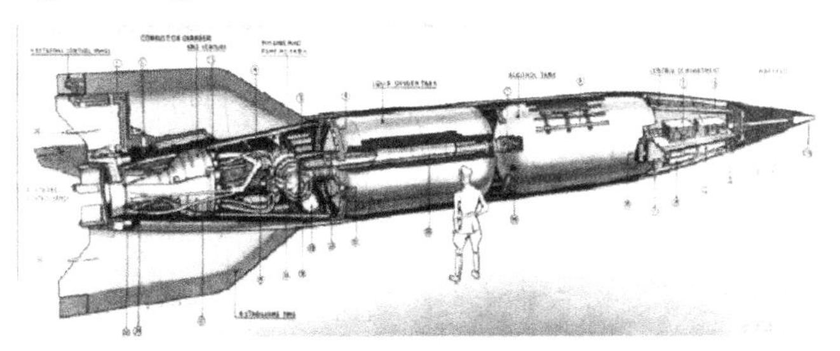

Thinking he would stop the Allies with his "secret weapon," Hitler used massive numbers of V2 rockets against Britain in the final months of the war.

V2 rocket production proved expensive (more so than the Manhattan Project which produced the atomic bomb) and redirected much of German's technical research and development. The program also used one third of Germany's fuel.

The real potential for the V2 rocket was realized after the war. It laid the foundation for American and Soviet nuclear missiles that could carry warheads thousands of miles. It also marked the dawn of space exploration and led to the "space race" between the U.S. and the Soviet Union.

In October 1946, just over a year after the war ended, a V2 missile launched by the United States took the first photograph of the earth from outer space.

Engineers in Nazi Germany were also the first to develop **jet aircraft** during the war. Due to Adolf Hitler's belief that Germany would win a quick victory, research and production of jet aircraft came too late to have any effect on the outcome of the war.

German Messerschmitt Me-262, the world's first operational jet aircraft

In many ways, German technology was far ahead of any other nation in the world during World War 2. American, Soviet, and British forces overcame superior German expertise by the sheer number of planes, tanks, and soldiers used in the European War.

By the end of the war the Allies had built more than four times as many machineguns and bomber aircraft and nearly ten times as many aircraft carriers as the Axis Powers.

Espionage and deception were also responsible for many of the Allied victories. Although Germany and Japan were active in the area of spying, neither achieved the same success as the Allies.

> Define
> **ESPIONAGE**
> The act or practice of spying or using spies to gather information

An inflatable dummy tank used to divert Germany's attention from Normandy

The Battle of Midway and the Soviet strategy of **maskirovka** (Russian for "disguise") proved the importance of secrets, deception, and espionage.

American and British leaders devised elaborate plans to distract the Nazis. As a result, the Germans moved troops and equipment to areas they were tricked into believing were intended targets. The most successful of these deceptions was **Operation Bodyguard**.

By the spring of 1944 Germany's high command knew that an Allied invasion was about to happen. American and British intelligence agents were busy determining the best place to attack and trying to keep the Germans from finding out.

After the plan was finalized to invade the beaches of France at Normandy, it became crucial to keep the location a secret to the Germans.

Operation Fortitude, one of the key components of Bodyguard, diverted Hitler's attention away from Normandy. The Allies focused on luring the Nazis to other parts of the northern coast of France. The Allies placed numerous fake inflatable airplanes, tanks, and landing craft in strategic places, mainly on the narrow passage of the English Channel at *Pas-de-Calais*. Hitler and his top commanders were also tricked into believing that General Patton would lead the attack.

Unknown to Hitler, most of the Nazi spies targeted against Britain had been captured and were working for the British to avoid prosecution.

Along with imaginary military divisions and phony Allied radio signals, the Nazi double agents relayed false information to the Germans. In addition, the British had cracked the German code.

The German secret code produced on a machine called **Enigma** had been reasonably deciphered by the Allies as the invasion of Europe approached.

Nazi Germany's secret code encryption machine, Enigma

Breaking the Nazi code was such an essential part of the Allied victory that Supreme Allied Commander Dwight D. Eisenhower considered it *"decisive"*.

With the success of *Operation Bodyguard* and confidence that Germany's war economy was crippled beyond repair, a date for the historic Allied invasion of Europe was set.

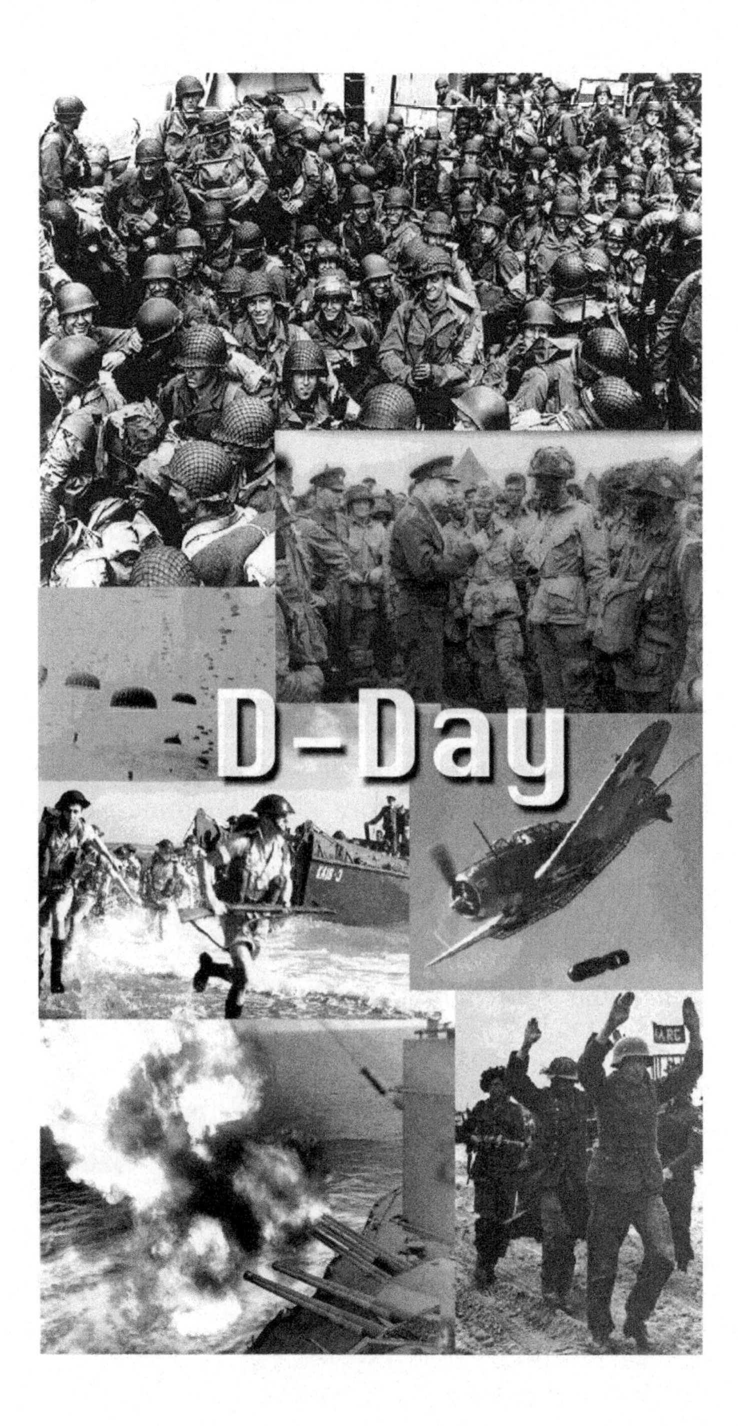
D-Day

Many dramatic events unfolded in June of 1944 as the Allied war effort focused on finally crushing the Axis Powers. On June 5th, Allied forces marched into Rome unopposed.

On the eastern front, the Soviet Union made great advances under the command of Marshal **Georgy Zhukov**, destroying German Army Group Center in a massive surprise attack. In the ensuing battle, the Nazi army was driven completely out of Soviet territory and lost more soldiers than in any other battle.

In the **Battle of the Philippine Sea**, the United States won a decisive victory. It was the largest aircraft carrier battle in history and resulted in a crushing defeat for the Japanese Imperial Navy.

Flight deck of the USS Lexington, Battle of the Philippine Sea June 1944

No other event in the Second World War got as much attention as **Operation Overlord** *(also known as D-Day)*. The invasion of Hitler's "Fortress Europe" on the beaches of Normandy, France remains one of the most notable battles in world history.

"Your enemy will fight savagely"

Destined for a mission so dangerous that Allied Commander Dwight Eisenhower warned his troops *"Your task will not be an easy one. Your enemy will fight savagely",* the enormous Allied flotilla crossed the English Channel on the morning of June 6th.

ABOVE: American troops crowded aboard a transport ship LEFT: British soldiers arm a warplane before launching for Normandy.

RIGHT: American bombers attacking the French coastline of Normandy at the outbreak of Operation Overlord, June 6th, 1944

With the success of Operation Bodyguard and other secret missions, the Germans were uncertain that the attacks on Normandy were even the main invasion force.

Due to bad weather, American bomber raids were not as effective as Eisenhower had hoped. **Paratroopers** from the 101st and 82nd U.S. Airborne Divisions were the first wave of the attack.

Define
PARATROOPER
A soldier that can reach targets by parachuting from an airplane

Dropped behind enemy lines, the paratroopers were on an extremely dangerous mission to secure bridges and towns and prevent the Nazis from sending reinforcements. Thick fog and powerful German anti-aircraft gunfire caused the 101st and 82nd to miss some of their targets. They suffered heavy losses but the mission proceeded successfully.

As the Allies reached the beaches, German opposition became fierce. The Americans attacked on the beaches code-named Omaha and Utah, while British and Canadian troops struck at Gold, Juno, and Sword.

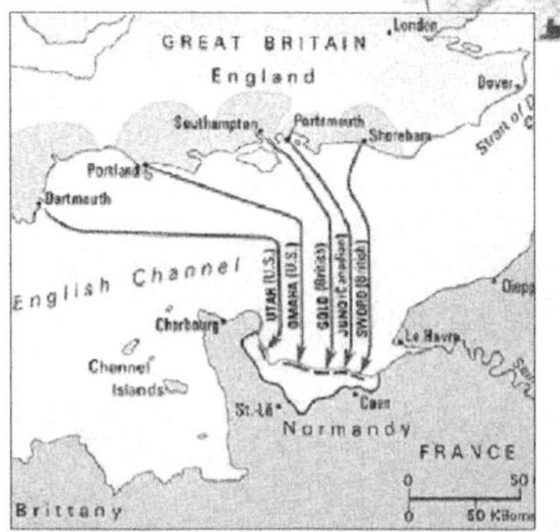

With a combined strength of over 160,000 men (to land on the beaches alone), the Allied attack on Normandy was the largest amphibious invasion in history, comprised of 5,000 sea going vessels and 11,000 aircraft.

Even with such an overwhelming force, the Nazi high command believed the D-Day invasion might be a diversion and did not redirect troops and equipment. Still, Allied casualties were heavy, especially at Omaha Beach where the Germans held on to the highly fortified cliffs.

By the end of the day, about 5,000 of the 50,000 American troops to land on Omaha had been killed or wounded. Because of the high casualty rate, the U.S. commanders, including General **Omar N. Bradley**, had almost called off the invasion soon after it began.

RIGHT: General Omar Bradley; BELOW: Reinforcements and supplies landing on the beaches of northern France following D-Day

However, small groups of brave soldiers, most without officers, persisted in fighting back the Nazis. With the support of naval bombardment, they eventually captured the beach and established a safe harbor.

German defenses were severely weakened, but the defenders regrouped and prevented the Allies from advancing inland as planned. In the days that followed, as more troops and supplies were brought in, the Germans finally withdrew.

Some of the Allied high command was upset about the lack of the U.S. Navy's involvement on D-Day. More lives could have been saved, they argued, had there been greater naval support.

Still, the mission was accomplished and the Allies gathered an enormous army in France. In the following weeks, Eisenhower appointed General Omar N. Bradley to command more than one million soldiers, the largest field command in history.

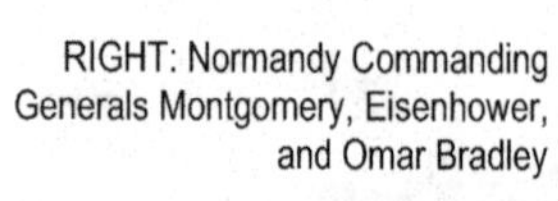

RIGHT: Normandy Commanding Generals Montgomery, Eisenhower, and Omar Bradley

The Normandy landings, like the Pacific Island campaigns against the Japanese Imperial Navy, proved to be a

decisive battle that paved the way for the war to be won. On July 10th 1944, just over a month after D-Day, Tokyo was bombed for the first time since the Doolittle Raid.

Not admitting defeat however, the Axis Powers were unconvinced the outcome of the Second World War had been decided. The fight was far from over. But with limited resources and a reduced fighting force, they were now clearly disadvantaged.

"D-Day" is a term the U.S. military used for any mission. It simply indicates the first day of an operation.

1944

August 25: *Allies liberate Paris, France*

October: *The largest naval battle in history is a huge victory for America against the Imperial Japanese Navy at the* ***Battle of Leyte Gulf***

November 7
President Franklin Roosevelt is elected for the fourth time. He remains the only president to ever serve more than 2 terms

Battle of the Bulge

As 1944 came to a close, Nazi Germany seemed doomed to defeat. The Allies had suffered some setbacks, but were pressing hard to conquer Hitler at his very doorstep. The defeat of Nazi Germany was quickly becoming a reality. Still, President Roosevelt and Winston Churchill knew their enemy would not go down without a fight.

In December the fight came in the form of a massive surprise German counter-offensive called the **Battle of the Bulge**.

General Patton's 3rd U.S. Army tanks were eagerly racing toward the western German border. Limited by his allowance of fuel and supplies, Patton was forced to wait.

Patton's 3rd U.S. Army was forced to slow down due to low supplies

Like Patton, General Bradley and British General Montgomery both demanded more supplies and reinforcements, but Eisenhower preferred a wide front with no favored "spearhead". This caused the line of advancing Allied troops and machinery to be stretched thin in some critical areas.

Supreme Allied Commander Dwight "Ike" Eisenhower discussing offensive plans with top U.S. military officials

Taking advantage of one of those weak spots, Hitler launched the counter-offensive on December 16, 1944. His goal was to divide the Americans and British, forcing them to negotiate a peace treaty on his terms. The Nazi counter-attack also exposed the Allied army's overconfidence.

The Battle of the Bulge was named for the nose shaped German offensive that stretched into the middle of the Allied front line.

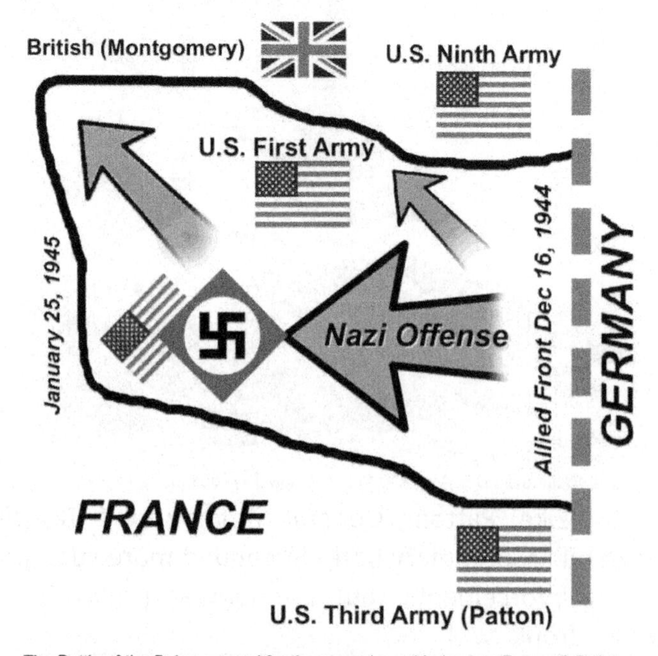

The Battle of the Bulge, named for the nose shaped bulge into France & Belgium

It took place in the Ardennes region of France and Belgium. Hitler acted on the bad weather, which allowed his tanks and troops to attack without being spotted or destroyed from the air.

The success of the Nazi offensive depended heavily on speed and secrecy. Information from the French Resistance was only reliable west of the German border. Deep inside Germany, Hitler's plan called for radio silence. Vital details were not relayed by Enigma, the famous Nazi code machine.

A major problem for the Nazis was lack of fuel. For the plan to succeed, the Germans relied on capturing American gas and oil supplies.

By Christmas Day 1944, the Germans had knocked the American advance off balance, breaking through the center of the western front.

Severely outnumbered by troops, tanks, and artillery, the American force within the "bulge" was overwhelmed. Nearly 90,000 U.S. soldiers were killed, wounded, captured, or missing in action. The Battle of the Bulge was America's largest and most deadly battle of World War 2.

ABOVE: American soldier struggles to operate a machine gun in icy conditions.

RIGHT: U.S. reinforcements race to resist the German counteroffensive, January 1945

In a famous incident, General Patton called on Chief Chaplain of the Third Army James O'Neill to prepare a prayer that the rain would stop so the American ground force could have air support:

"Almighty and most merciful Father, we humbly beseech Thee, of Thy great goodness, to restrain these immoderate rains with which we have had to contend. Grant us fair weather for Battle. Graciously hearken to us as soldiers who call upon Thee that, armed with Thy power, we may advance from victory to victory, and crush the oppression and wickedness of our enemies and establish Thy justice among men and nations."

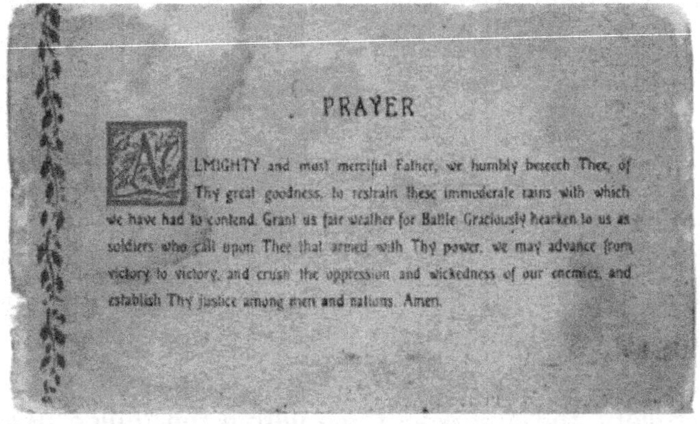

PRAYER

ALMIGHTY and most merciful Father, we humbly beseech Thee, of Thy great goodness, to restrain these immoderate rains with which we have had to contend. Grant us fair weather for Battle. Graciously hearken to us as soldiers who call upon Thee that armed with Thy power, we may advance from victory to victory, and crush the oppression and wickedness of our enemies, and establish Thy justice among men and nations. Amen.

ABOVE: A copy of Patton's prayer distributed to soldiers during the Battle of the Bulge

Although the Allied air offensives against Germany had effectively stopped the **Luftwaffe**, the terrible weather had grounded American and British air forces. Patton was so grieved by the enemy's chance for victory that he complained,

"The poor visibility and the continual rains have completely paralyzed my air forces on the ground. But worse still, my reconnaissance aircraft have not taken to the air in fourteen days, and I do not have the slightest idea what is happening behind the German lines."

The New York Times.

LATE CITY EDITION

GERMANS SWEEP WEST THROUGH LUXEMBOURG; REPORT PATTON ATTACKING ON SOUTH FLANK; EISENHOWER URGES GREATEST ALLIED EFFORT

MAYOR DEMANDS U.S. ACT AT ONCE ON MEAT CRISIS

ROOSEVELT URGES HOMEFOLKS TO BACK SOLDIERS AT FRONT

GERMAN TOWN REDUCED TO RUBBLE AFTER SHELLING BY BOTH SIDES

CITY BUDGET SUIT UPHELD ON APPEAL

Commander in Chief Hails

Back home in the United States, church leaders across the land called on Americans to pray as well. The fourth Christmas after Pearl Harbor was plagued by the fear of more American deaths in the Battle of the Bulge.

United States government poster depicting the Axis view of religion in America

President Roosevelt also asked for Americans to lift their voices in prayer in his regular national radio address to the country:

"Many people have urged that I call the nation into a single day of special prayer. But because the road is long and the desire is great, I ask that our people devote themselves in a continuance of prayer. As we rise to each new day, and again when each day is spent, let words of prayer be on our lips."

As the New Year approached, Americans once again felt the disappointment of another setback and had little to celebrate. But the president and his top leaders knew the tide of the war had turned in their favor.

Heavy rain and fog masking their arrival, a quarter million strong Nazi force pushed through the thin American front along an 85-mile line. The U.S. First Army bore the brunt of the assault with devastating results.

On December 23rd— to the delight of the Allies and the surprise of weather forecasters—Patton's prayer was answered. The rain ceased and the skies cleared, allowing the Allied planes to launch by the thousands.

In planning the Battle of the Bulge, Hitler's greatest fear was clear skies. The Nazi counter-attack was beaten back as the Allied advance continued. Hitler's gamble failed, costing Germany severely.

Casualties were also great for the U.S. and American morale was damaged. Eisenhower and his commanders learned a valuable lesson about under-estimating Hitler's will and ability to wage war.

But with vast losses on the western front and an enormous invasion by the Soviets in the east, the once mighty Nazi war machine was all but finished.

The Battle of the Bulge would go down in history as Germany's epic last stand, yet Hitler still refused to surrender. Even with the probability of substantial civilian deaths, the Nazis fought to the bitter end. Some top Nazi leaders tried to stop Hitler by plotting to assassinate him and overthrow the government before it was too late. One such effort called "Operation Valkyrie" involved German Lieutenant Colonel **Claus von Stauffenberg**.

Operation Valkyrie, a complex plan that would eventually fail, consisted of several key phases that required accurate timing.

Define
ASSASSINATE
To kill a leader or person of influence, usually for political reasons

Although the assassination attempt involved many high-ranking Nazi political and military officials, it was kept top secret by the *German Resistance*, allowing von Stauffenberg to actually carry a bomb concealed in a briefcase into Hitler's headquarters.

Colonel von Stauffenberg

On July 20th, 1944 Colonel von Stauffenberg slid the bomb under a sturdy desk in the conference room where Hitler and key military leaders were gathered. Colonel von Stauffenberg then left the room to answer a phone call. The call was planned as an excuse for von Stauffenberg to escape after the bomb's timer was activated.

Four people were killed in the blast, but Hitler survived with minor injuries. Colonel von Stauffenberg managed to escape, but was arrested along with over 7,000 other suspects in the next several months. Nearly five thousand were executed, including von Stauffenberg.

Even Germany's most famous general, Erwin Rommel, was suspected of taking part in the conspiracy to kill Hitler. Because Rommel was a national hero, Hitler wanted to get rid of him quietly.

In exchange for a promise that his family would be safe, Rommel agreed to commit suicide. The public was told that he died of previous battle wounds. He was given a state funeral with full military honors.

General Rommel's funeral procession, October 1944

There had always been a circle of top-level German officials who opposed Hitler. Rommel, who was never accused of any war crimes, directly disobeyed Hitler's orders to kill civilians, Jews, and captured enemy prisoners.

[Rommel] "deserves our respect, because although a loyal German soldier, he came to hate Hitler and all his works, and took part in the conspiracy to rescue Germany by displacing the maniac and tyrant. For this he paid the forfeit of his life." -Winston Churchill

Field Marshal Erwin Johannes Eugen Rommel

WOMEN OF WAR

German Nurse fitting Children with Gas Masks

We Can Do It!

British Woman Auxilary Pilot

American Factory Workers

"Tokyo Rose"

Soviet Women Defy Nazis

Female Nurses at Normandy after D-Day

Women of War

In the twenty years between World War One and World War Two, society changed in many ways. Technology, especially in aircraft and automobiles, took huge leaps. The Great Depression altered the financial situation of millions of people. Radio and motion pictures ushered in a new period of mass communication.

The role of women also changed dramatically after the First World War ended in 1918. Before 1920, women were not allowed to vote. The vast majority of students, jobholders, and business owners were men, while their wives stayed home to run the household.

American Nurse circa 1920

If women worked outside the home it was because of poverty, and typically worked at jobs regarded as "woman's work" like teaching, cleaning, and nursing.

Before the attack on Pearl Harbor in December of 1941, women held less than 10% of manufacturing jobs. By 1944, that percentage had more than tripled. With so many men fighting overseas and the increased demand for warplanes, ships, and other weaponry, American women were encouraged to work.

One of the most famous jobs that women performed during the Second World War was inserting rivets on airplane parts.

The iconic image of "**Rosie the Riveter**" became a common symbol of women in the wartime workplace.

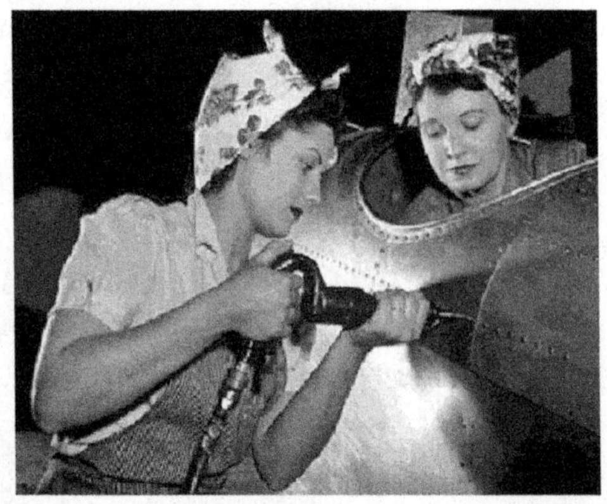

Not all the jobs were in manufacturing, however. Men vacated nearly every segment of the workplace, and women felt it was their patriotic duty to step in.

American women also joined the military by the hundreds of thousands, serving on the home front and overseas in such units as the **WAVES** (a

U.S. Navy division) and the **Women's Army Corps** (WAC), the women's branch of the United States Army. For the first time in history, women became commissioned officers in the U.S. armed forces.

All military nurses were females during World War 2, and the United States government recruited over 60,000.

Every nation involved in the war needed women to fill the demand when men went into combat. The Soviet Union allowed women to fight on the front lines as soldiers. Nazi Germany and Japan used women in factories, communications, and propaganda.

Workers assembling B29 bombers

Women played a role in espionage and both the Allies and the Axis Powers employed numerous female spies.

"Tokyo Rose" was the generic name given by American servicemen for a small group of Japanese radio personalities. The women spoke in English on the airwaves to troops in the Pacific. Their intention was to discourage the servicemen's fighting spirit by telling them they should be at home with their families and girlfriends.

Japanese women working at an ammunition factory

President Roosevelt's wife, First Lady **Eleanor Roosevelt**, was credited with elevating the role of women and minorities in all social circles. After she visited American troops in the South Pacific, Admiral William Halsey, Jr. remarked, *"She alone accomplished more good than any other person, or any groups of civilians, who had passed through my area."*

United States servicemen raise the American flag at Iwo Jima, February 1945

As the New Year rolled in, Allied momentum was in full force. American, British, and Canadian troops pressed hard to cross the German border on the western front. By January 1945, Soviet troops had liberated most of Poland and were rumbling into Germany from the east.

Forced from his headquarters in Eastern Europe, Hitler secluded himself in a Berlin bunker along with his companion **Eva Braun**.

On February 23 U.S. forces raised the American flag on the island of **Iwo Jima**, preparing the way for an Allied invasion of mainland Japan.

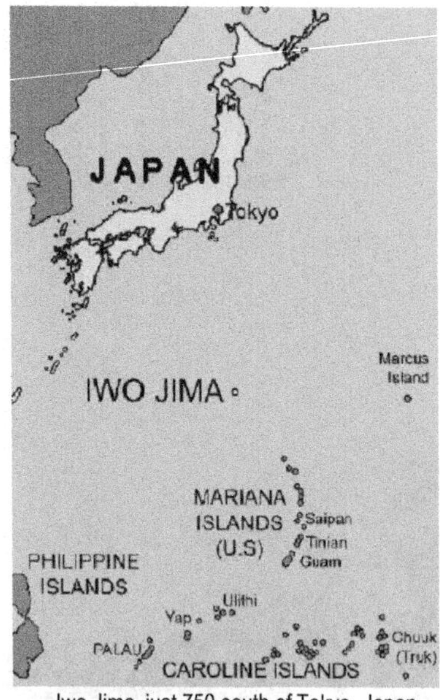

Iwo Jima, just 750 south of Tokyo, Japan

Just 750 miles south of Tokyo, Iwo Jima was one of the last Pacific Islands to fall. Japan's ability to make war was quickly being immobilized by Allied attacks and blockades. But American military planners had never believed it would be simple to beat the Japanese, even with a massive **amphibious** invasion.

Define
AMPHIBIOUS
(Military): Refers to an operation combining naval and land troops and equipment

The next crucial step in planning such an invasion would be the capture of **Okinawa**, a large island barely 350 miles south of Japan.

LEFT: An American submarine officer using the periscope to track enemy activity

Both sides realized the importance of Okinawa and were preparing for a deadly showdown. American planners knew that Japanese defense strategy meant never surrendering. At Okinawa both would face their greatest challenge of the Pacific War.

Typhoon of Steel

United States Marine firing a Thompson sub-machinegun at enemy garrison on Okinawa

Codenamed Operation Iceberg, the **Battle of Okinawa** was referred to as the "typhoon of steel" because of the severe destruction of the conflict.

More lives were lost on both sides than any other battle in the Pacific, and civilian casualties were staggering as well. All told, more than 250,000 people lost their lives.

Unlike many other islands where major battles took place in the Pacific, Okinawa had a large civilian population of around 300,000, and as many as half were reported being killed or wounded as a result of the hostilities.

Beginning on Easter Sunday April 1, 1945, the Battle of Okinawa raged until mid-June. Perhaps more than any other battle, it served to demonstrate the stubborn determination of the Japanese people.

Plans to invade mainland Japan were revised to allow for the fact that Japanese troops and civilians were simply unwilling to surrender.

Although Allied forces had the advantage in almost every way, the Japanese balanced the fight with sheer determination. With fuel supplies and ammunition almost depleted, Japanese civilians were told to take up bamboo spears if necessary.

As amphibious assaults became more common toward the end of the war, Allied forces had to get creative. A major problem was transporting troops and supplies further inland from the beach. One solution was the DUKW vehicle. Designed as a combination of a boat and a truck, the DUKW, or "duck" as they were known, could travel on sea or land. Unique features like six wheels, a propeller, and boat hull gave the DUKW the ability to perform amphibious duties like no other vehicle.

With more troops and a larger flotilla and air force than even the Normandy landings on D-Day, the amphibious assault on Okinawa was the largest armada ever assembled in the history of warfare.

Just as the Battle of the Bulge turned out to be Germany's last major conflict a few weeks earlier, Okinawa would be Japan's final epic battle.

Generals Buckner and Ushijima, the top commanders, were both killed at Okinawa

Japanese losses were enormous. Nearly 8,000 aircraft were destroyed. Because of their policy of fighting to the last man, around 100,000 troops were killed, about 85% of the fighting force.

Also killed at Okinawa were the two top regional commanders of *both* armies, Imperial Japanese Army General **Mitsuru Ushijima** and Four-Star General **Simon Bolivar Buckner**, Jr. (the highest ranking American officer killed in World War 2 by enemy fire) *and* the top admiral of the Japanese naval force on Okinawa, **Minoru Ōta**.

Legendary American news reporter **Ernie Pyle**, who was known for his bravery and often reported war stories from the front lines, was also killed at Okinawa by Japanese gunfire.

Army Lt. Col. Joseph B. Coolidge, who was next to Pyle when he was killed, said, *"(the) enlisted men have lost their best friend."*

The amphibious assault on Okinawa was the largest armada ever assembled

Kamikazi pilot aims for a U.S. Navy vessel

Perhaps because it occurred so close to the end of the war, the Battle of Okinawa was overshadowed by other major conflicts like Normandy and the North Africa campaign. Yet the "typhoon of steel" remains one of the largest, deadliest, and most tragic military operations in history.

From Time to Eternity

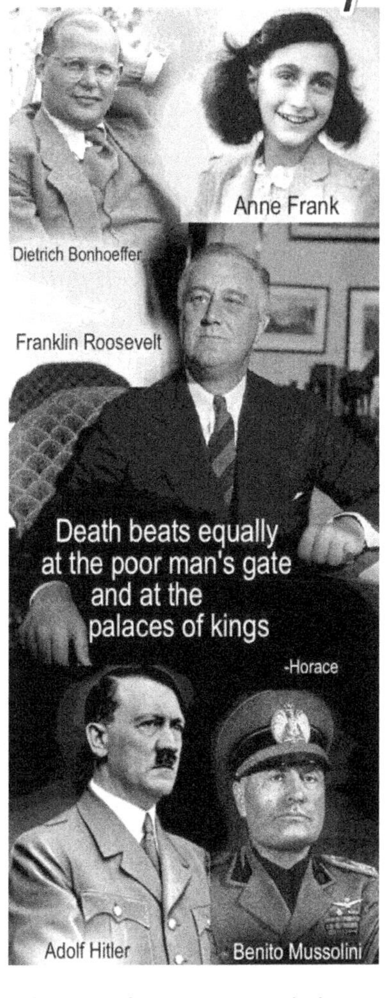

As the United States and her allies prepared for the final deadly drive into Germany and Japan in the spring of 1945, some of the war's most famous lives would come to an unfortunate end.

No one really knew **Anne Frank** until long after the war. Bright, friendly, and innocent, Anne was taken prisoner by the Nazis and died March 12 at the age of fifteen. She kept a diary of her life as a victim of the Nazi Holocaust. Her diary was published two years after the war and has since sold millions of copies and been printed in over 60 languages.

A brilliant Christian Bible scholar and patriot, **Dietrich Bonhoeffer** risked his life to openly criticize Hitler's atrocities as a pastor in Nazi Germany. He was hanged on April 9th, just two weeks before he would have been liberated from the concentration camp where he had been imprisoned.

Three of the top political leaders of World War 2 all died in April 1945, ironically within days of the end of the war in Europe.

President Franklin Delano Roosevelt *died suddenly on April 12. President Roosevelt had led the nation longer than any other president, from the Great Depression and literally through the Second World War. He was 63.*

Benito Mussolini*, the once powerful Fascist leader, captured by his own countrymen while trying to escape Italy, was executed on April 29th. All Italian forces formally surrendered the same day. He was 61.*

Adolf Hitler *committed suicide on April 30th, ten days after his birthday. Along with his companion Eva Braun, whom he had married the night before, Hitler was hiding from Russian troops in an underground Berlin bunker. He was 56.*

For death is no more than a turning of us over from time to time to eternity.

~William Penn

The Battle of Berlin

The last Allied European offensive would be fought in the very heart of Germany, the capital city of Berlin. Predicting heavy losses from "friendly fire" if the American and Soviet armies invaded the city from both sides, General Eisenhower ordered a halt on the race to Berlin.

On April 16, American troops stopped just sixty miles west of

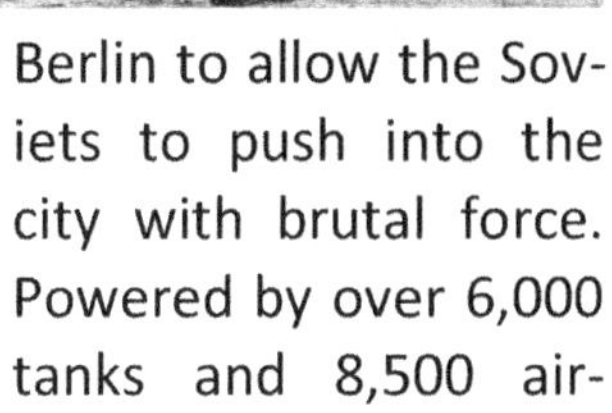

Berlin to allow the Soviets to push into the city with brutal force. Powered by over 6,000 tanks and 8,500 aircraft, the Soviets rallied an army of two and a half million soldiers to storm the last stronghold of Nazi resistance.

Hidden deep in a bunker underneath the streets of Berlin, Adolf Hitler struggled for a final desperate opportunity to alter the inescapable outcome. As the deafening blast of Soviet artillery thundered above him, Hitler surely must have contemplated how the war could have ended differently. Before the invasion of Poland, Germany had been at the pinnacle of military supremacy.

In all of history no other nation had amassed an army and navy as loyal and as well equipped in such a short time. Never before had the world seen a man so obsessed with power and revenge. Never before had the world been plunged into destruction on such an unimaginable scale.

Maybe, in his final hours, Hitler realized that his generals might have been right. Had he taken their advice and not invaded the Soviet Union or declared war on the United States and concentrated on defeating England instead of opening new fronts, the war could have ended in his favor.

Ten years earlier, Adolf Hitler had stunned the world with the magnitude of his accomplishments, such as the 1936 Berlin Olympic games, which featured the first television broadcast in history. Now, alone with only a few close associates by his side, all of his dreams were caving in on him.

By April 29th, Berlin was completely surrounded and cut off from the rest of Germany. The Reich Chancellery (including Hitler's bunker) was shelled intensely, and for the first time Hitler would openly admit the war to be lost.

Polish troops storm Berlin, May 2nd

As Germany crumbled around them, the last defenders of the Reich Chancellery informed their Fuhrer that they would run out of ammunition within 24 hours.

The next day, rather than being made "a spectacle of" as he said, Adolf Hitler and his wife Eva killed themselves. Two days later, the commanding General of the last defenders, General Helmuth Weidling, surrendered to the Soviet Red Army.

American and Soviet troops link up for the first time in Germany, late April 1945

Some German troops still fought the Soviets as they retreated west with the intention of surrendering to the Americans. But Eisenhower demanded an unconditional surrender from German High Command and threatened to close the lines to any German soldiers seeking refuge.

Fighting continued for a few days, street-to-street, even house-to-house before the formal declaration of surrender, signed by Germany's Chief of Armed Forces High Command Alfred Jodl on May 7th, 1945. After six long years, the war in Europe was officially over.

Berlin, and much of Europe, had been reduced to ash and ruins. But even though the Pacific War was still blazing, the entire world took a moment to celebrate the news of Germany's surrender.

V-E Day

"Victory in Europe Day", or **V-E Day** for short, was a public holiday held on May 8, 1945 to celebrate the end of the war in Europe. Millions of people gathered in the streets of London, New York, and Moscow to rejoice.

Because so many had paid the ultimate sacrifice and died to bring Hitler's Third Reich to an end and millions of unarmed civilians had been killed, the holiday was very emotional for millions of families.

In the United States, as the nation grieved the death of President Roosevelt, the Victory in Europe Day celebration fell on new president Harry Truman's 61st birthday.

British Prime Minister Winston Churchill waves to the crowd on V-E Day

President **Harry Truman** dedicated Victory in Europe Day to the memory of the former president, saying that his only wish was *"that Franklin D. Roosevelt had lived to witness this day."*

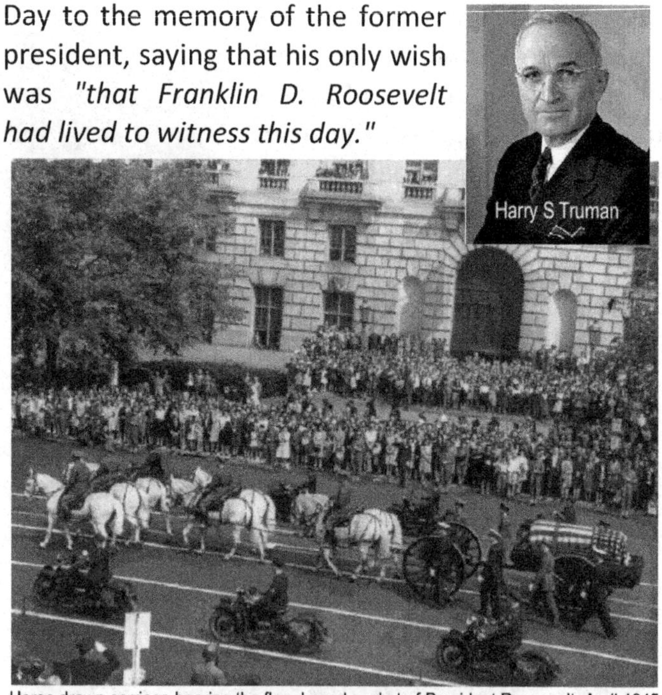

Horse drawn carriage bearing the flag draped casket of President Roosevelt, April 1945

A Restless Peace

At the top levels of British and American command, V-E Day was marred by Joseph Stalin's apparent unwillingness to keep his agreement. Eastern Europe had been swallowed up by the Soviet Union as the Red Army forced its way toward Germany.

Winston Churchill was furious that American troops had stopped and allowed the Soviets to enter Berlin, and after Germany's defeat, the British prime minister was more suspicious of the Russians than ever. To plan the fate of post-war Europe, Churchill, Truman, and Stalin met at the **Potsdam Conference** in occupied Germany in July of 1945.

Churchill had hoped that President Truman would join him in standing up to Stalin, even going as far as suggesting military action to force the Soviets out of Poland and other countries under Soviet control. But during the conference, Churchill faced re-election in Britain and, to the surprise of many, lost to his challenger **Clement Attlee**.

The "Big 3" at Potsdam

With Roosevelt and Churchill gone, Stalin was able to negotiate with the western allies more on his terms. America and Britain were beginning to understand that the Soviet Union had intentions of spreading communism in Europe, but no one was ready to start another war. Truman still had to defeat the Japanese, and Attlee was elected to focus more on social problems inside England.

Decisions made by the U.S. and Russia leading to Hitler's defeat would cause millions of Eastern Europeans to endure communist control for the next fifty years. The Allies divided Germany—East Germany under communist Russian control and West Germany occupied by American forces.

Because of Nazi Germany's influence, the entire world experienced great change. From the 1950's through the 1990's the United States and the Soviet Union struggled against each other in a "**Cold War**". The term was used to describe the tension caused by the conflicting beliefs and political activity of both nations. After 1949, both had nuclear bombs, and the anxiety only escalated.

With the help of rocket technologies that German scientists like **Wernher von Braun** had developed during World War 2, the United States and the Soviet Union became engaged in an epic struggle that even reached outer space.

LEFT: Werner von Braun in Nazi Germany, 1941 and with President John F. Kennedy in 1962

Fearing harsh treatment from the Soviets, Dr. von Braun, who was called the "Father of Rocket Science", surrendered to the United States after Germany's defeat. He became extremely important to NASA and the American space program.

The Soviets and Americans competed in a all out "space race" to launch a man into orbit and eventually land on the moon. In 1959, less than fifteen years after World War 2, the Soviets sent a spacecraft to photograph the far side of the moon.

LEFT TO RIGHT: 1961- Russian Yuri Gagarin, the 1st human in outer space; 1969- Neil Armstrong, American, the 1st man to walk on the moon; The U.S. Space Shuttle Columbia on its maiden voyage, April 12, 1981

German scientific development had given the Nazis a competitive edge early in the war. Some historians contend that Adolf Hitler could have used technology more to his advantage had he listened to the advice of his senior military staff.

Although a German scientist built the first working jet plane, Hitler had not planned for a long war and saw no need to pursue jet aircraft development until late in the war.

American military personnel view an atomic bomb test

Another disturbing scenario is the possibility that the Nazis might have developed the first **atomic bomb** before the Manhattan Project. But once again, Hitler did not give the German atomic program priority and Germany fell behind the United States and Britain in research and development.

Although the Nazis and the Japanese joined forces in an effort to produce nuclear weapons, America had invested more heavily in research and was ready to put atomic warfare to use against both Axis Powers before Germany was defeated.

On July 16th 1945, the **Manhattan Project** successfully tested an atomic bomb. The explosion could be heard for 200 miles. A blind woman actually saw the flash that lit up the predawn New Mexico sky, 150 miles from the test site.

Top-secret cooperation among thousands of engineers, scientists, and technicians led to the creation of a frightening new weapon that could quickly end the Pacific War. The program was so secretive, President Truman had not known about it while he was still vice president.

Having arrived at the Potsdam Conference in occupied Germany with Churchill and Stalin, President Truman was anxious to hear of the test results. After learning that the test was successful, Truman hinted to Stalin about the bomb. Due to Soviet spies inside the American nuclear program, however, Stalin already knew, even before Truman did.

With the weight of the world on his shoulders, the new president was faced with the most important decision of his life. Later, Eleanor Roosevelt, the former First Lady, said that Truman *"made the only choice he could... to avoid tremendous sacrifice of American lives."*

Less than four months after being sworn in as the 34th President of the United States, Harry Truman decided to use the atomic bomb against Japan.

Code-named **Operation Downfall**, a full-scale invasion of Japan to be led by General Douglas MacArthur and Admiral Chester Nimitz, was already scheduled to begin November 1st, 1945. It would have been the largest invasion in history.

Five Star General of the Army Douglas MacArthur returns to the Philippines, 1945

Because of the fanatical loyalty of the Japanese population to the Emperor, fighting to the death by the defenders would be assured. Even children were instructed to die fighting.

The Japanese were reported to have over 10,000 airplanes, almost all to be used by *kamikaze* suicide pilots. Casualties would be extremely high on both sides and the war might go on for years, costing billions of dollars.

Even after the decision was made to drop the atomic bomb on Japan, Operation Downfall was still considered to be necessary. Some top military planners thought the Japanese would not surrender and as many as fifteen atomic bombs were added to the plan to ensure victory.

The mission to drop the first atom bomb remained top secret, even to the crewmembers of the B-29 Superfortress that carried the device in its payload. Only after takeoff of the B29 "**Enola Gay**" on the morning of August 6th, 1945 was the aim of the assignment revealed to the crew.

Pilot Colonel Paul Tibbets (center) and crew of the Enola Gay, named for Tibbets' mother

LEFT: "Little Boy", codename for the atomic bomb dropped on Hiroshima; BELOW: The Enola Gay in flight to Japan

"The atom bomb was no 'great decision.' It was merely another powerful weapon in the arsenal of righteousness", President Truman would later say.

The city of Hiroshima in southern Japan had been chosen as the primary target because of the large concentration of military supplies and troops stationed to guard against an Allied invasion. On July 26th the Allies proposed the conditions of Japan's surrender at the Potsdam Conference, including a warning of "prompt and utter destruction". The Japanese leaders rejected the offer.

As the bomb fell over Hiroshima and exploded, we saw an entire city disappear. I wrote in my log the words, "My God, what have we done?"

Capt. Robert Lewis, co-pilot of the Enola Gay

ABOVE: Hiroshima, before and after the atomic bomb explosion.
LEFT: Mushroom cloud rising 11 miles above the city in ten minutes

On August 6th at 08:15, "Little Boy" was released over Hiroshima. Forty-five seconds later 80,000 people were dead. 60,000 more would later die from injuries and radiation poisoning.

Japanese military and government leaders including Emperor Hirohito were shocked by the devastation. Yet they still were unwilling to surrender, at least on the terms offered at the Potsdam Conference.

Growing impatient with Japan's reluctance to surrender, President Harry Truman offered another chance, saying, *"If they do not now accept our terms, they may expect a rain of ruin from the air, the like of which has never been seen on this earth."*

Soviet troops roll into Manchuria after declaring war on Japan, August 9, 1945

Top-level officials met in Tokyo to discuss the situation. Some were ready to give in to the Allies' demands while others insisted on fighting till the end.

In the middle of the discussions, on August 9th, they learned that the Soviet Union had declared war and suddenly invaded Manchuria, in occupied northern China, forcing the Japanese leadership to reconsider their circumstances. Like Germany, Japan had signed a **Neutrality** Pact with the Soviet Union early in the war.

Define

NEUTRALITY

(Military): Staying out of a conflict by not taking either side in a war

With the double shock of the atom bombing of Hiroshima and Soviet Russia declaring war, Japan was forced to quickly decide to either surrender or face the consequences.

More than one million Soviet soldiers quickly defeated the overwhelmed Japanese forces and moved into Korea. Another devastating blow came later that same day when the U.S. dropped a second atom bomb on the city of **Nagasaki**. Unable to come to a mutual agreement, the Japanese war council called on Hirohito to decide what to do. It would be six days before he announced his decision.

PEACE ON EARTH

In the meantime, on August 14th, Truman ordered the largest conventional bombing of the Pacific War on Japanese targets. Japanese citizens were also growing weary of the war. Civil unrest added to the unlikelihood of Japan negotiating more favorable terms.

Finally, on August 15th at 12:00 noon Japanese time, the Emperor's proclamation of Japan's surrender was broadcast to his nation.

American sailors gathered around a radio rejoicing at the news of Japan's surrender

American Armed Forces personnel celebrate victory August 15th, 1945

News of the announcement sent millions of people out into the streets to rejoice that the Second World War had ended. In Britain, the holiday was called V-J Day, or "Victory Over Japan" Day.

V-J Day was officially celebrated in the U.S. on September 2nd, the day when Japanese leaders signed the formal unconditional surrender aboard the battleship **USS Missouri**, anchored in Tokyo Bay.

LEFT: The Japanese delegation arrives for the ceremony

Aftermath

U.S. Air Force Sabre jet aircraft, Korean War 1950

In the months following the Second World War, governments changed, soldiers returned home, but everyone had a sense that the world would never be the same.

Many Axis political leaders and officers, such as Gestapo chief **Heinrich Himmler** who supervised the Nazi extermination camps, committed suicide rather than face certain execution.

Following the war, numerous German war criminals were brought to justice at the **Nuremberg Trials**.

Just weeks after the war was over, General **George S. Patton** died from injuries he received in an automobile accident.

Supreme Allied Commander General **Dwight D. Eisenhower** won the 1952 election to become the 34th President of the United States. He was re-elected in 1956 and led the nation in a time of peace and prosperity.

Emperor Hirohito was shielded from responsibility for any war crimes and was never charged. General MacArthur insisted that Hirohito retain his throne, and in a controversial decision he was allowed to stay in power. Though his authority was more limited, he remained Japan's emperor until his death on January 7th, 1989.

The fight over the division of Germany continued in June of 1948 as the Soviets blocked all access to the west in Berlin. The U.S. responded by flying in tons of food and supplies before the **Berlin Blockade** was finally lifted in May 1949.

The United States and the Soviet Union became the dominant world "superpowers". The Soviet-backed communist revolution in China after the Second World War alarmed Americans with a fear that communism would spread.

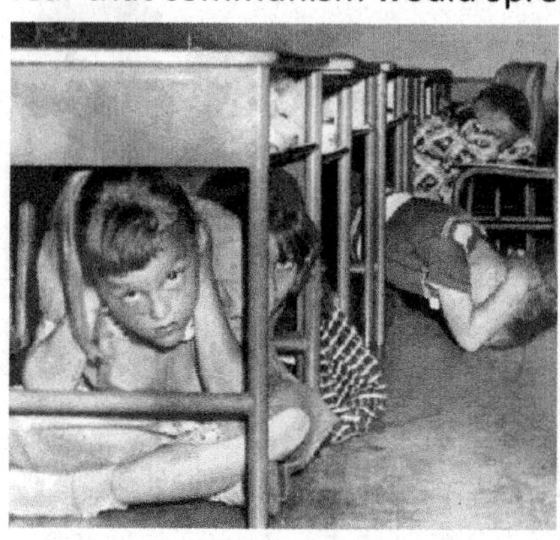

In fear of a nuclear war, U.S. school children were trained in "duck and cover" drills

Just five years after World War 2, American troops went to war against the communist forces in Korea. It was the first major conflict where jet aircraft faced off in battle. Because of the threat of

nuclear war, it was also the first "limited" war leaving Korea divided. Hostilities linger to this day.

World War 2 also brought awareness of racism to the forefront of the American conscience, birthing the Civil Rights Movement in the 1950s.

African-Americans had served their country bravely during the war, and many black soldiers returned home unhappier than ever about racial discrimination.

Benjamin Oliver Davis, Sr. became the 1st African-American General in the U.S. Army in 1940 and was awarded the Distinguished Service Medal for his service in World War 2. His son, Benjamin O. Davis, Jr. became the 1st black General in the U.S. Air Force in 1954

Dedicated on January 15th, 1943, the Pentagon Building, headquarters of the U.S. military, was the only building in Virginia until the late 1960s where blacks and whites were allowed to use the same restrooms and cafeteria.

Touring the facility after the official ground-breaking on September 11, 1941, President Franklin D. Roosevelt objected to separate restrooms for "whites" and "colored". Consequently, the Pentagon has twice as many restrooms than it needs.

By Executive Order 9981 issued on July 26, 1948, President Truman ended racial discrimination in the U.S. military. Because of this, great strides were made toward segregation and equality for minorities in the latter part of the 20th century.

Out of the ashes and rubble

of the Second World War, Germany and Japan would be rebuilt and became powerful nations once again. By the early 21st century, Japan and Germany had become the third and fourth strongest economies in the world, respectively, behind the United States and China.

The magnitude of destruction and the development of powerful new weapons during World War 2 caused leaders of all nationalities to come together in an effort to prevent a third world war and atrocities like the Holocaust. The **United Nations** (UN) was officially formed in 1945, just a few months after the war. Inscribed on a wall near the United Nations Headquarters building in New York City is a verse from the Bible:

"...they shall beat their swords into plowshares, and their spears into pruning hooks: Nation shall not lift up sword against nation, neither shall they learn war any more."

(Isaiah 2:4)

Made in the USA
Las Vegas, NV
13 April 2021

21327949R00095